I Only Cry *At* Night

Living
with
Sickle Cell Disease

P. Allen Jones

This book may be purchased in bulk for educational, business,
fund-raising or sales promotional use. For information, please
email info@pallenjones.com.

Scripture quotations are taken from the King James Version of
the Bible. Public domain.

Jones, P. Allen
I Only Cry at Night, living with Sickle Cell Disease

ISBN-13: 978-1463573645
-10: 1463573642

Printed in the United States of America

DEDICATION

This book is dedicated to all those brave people living with Sickle Cell Disease who also cry at night.

Yea, Though I walk through the valley of the shadow of death,

I will fear no evil;

for thou art with me;

thy rod and thy staff comfort me…

Psalm 23:4

CONTENTS

ACKNOWLEDGEMENTS

I always knew God was with me, leading me, comforting me, and loving me through all my pain. I acknowledge Jesus Christ first and foremost for His gift of mercy, which endures forever.

I thank my husband and children for being the joys of my life. Their love has inspired me to dream past my physical limitations, and their encouragement has been the fire that warms my heart.

To my sisters and brothers who lived this journey along side me. We were in the same family, but our experience was different. This is my experience and I chose to change your names to protect your own experience. Thank you for understanding my pain while enduring your own.

To my herbalist, Rev. Robert Jones, who taught me how to use God's gift of herbs to care for my body in a natural way. And, to the many physicians who encouraged me to take ownership of my own care. Specifically, to Dr. Kimberly Reece, who showed compassion when I needed it most and understood my lifelong journey of pain. Thank God for healers!

Lastly, to my mother and father who didn't have a manual on how to raise sick children, but taught me lifelong lessons. One of which is; everyone makes mistakes, even parents.

1
THE BEGINNING

My earliest memory is my fourth birthday, when my mother gave me a red velvet dress, the most beautiful dress I'd ever seen. The waist flared out around me like a fairy princess gown. The collar looped around my neck framing a face that couldn't stop smiling. A large silk ribbon belt finished the look by being tied in a bow along my back. If ever there was a chance I'd look like a child who was loved, on this day I was.

My mother, an unusually beautiful light-skinned woman, dreamed of being an actress and model, but instead at seventeen got married to my father when she became pregnant. She watched her dreams disappear as one child grew into a family of 14 children. I was number 12, and I rarely had a moment alone with her—there were too many kids crying, kids fighting, kids hiding, and kids lost.

Most of our birthdays passed unacknowledged, but this birthday was different. She had given me the velvet dress—and a day with her, alone.

Together, I remember, we walked toward the bus stop near our house. I nearly stumbled from repeatedly looking down, pleased with my soft velvety dress and shiny black shoes. I sang to myself, moving my hips to make the dress dance. My mother didn't notice my small acts of vanity, and as the bus pulled up, we both stepped on for my first bus ride ever.

The film she took me to see was The *Itsy-Bitsy Polka-Dot Bikini*, and, even at four, I knew it wasn't a film for a child. But I was entranced by the theater, with its towering gold columns rising with engraved figures of angels on top. The seats were made of the same crimson velvet as my dress, and the screen was as tall as the building itself. I looked at people sitting near us, wondering who they were and where they lived. I was usually lost in a crowd of children, but this moment was rare and I cherished every minute of it. That day, alone with my mother, I knew for the first time what it was to be happy.

How different that moment was from the time I first discovered pain.

At four years old, I had grown into a girl who knew she was going to be a tap-dancing star. I adored black-and-white films with Judy Garland dancing in top-hat and tails. My family had grown accustom to ignoring

2

me as I took to the living room, with its glossy oak floor, reviving Judy's dance routines in my shiny black shoes. That living room floor was not only my stage. For me, it was an escape to Judy's time, with her audience showering me with applause as I turned and slid across the floor.

But one day, while tapping and clicking toward the stairs, I slid across the floor and landed right on top of the gas heater mounted in the center of the floor of the living room. My left thigh sizzled against it like bacon.

At first, I felt no pain. The day was very cold. It took a moment for my mind to register that the red-hot heater was frying my skin. I sat shocked, unable to move. By the time someone pulled me off, a patch of my skin remained on the cast iron grill, dissolving. My mother, as she did with any injury, simply ran cold water and smeared Vaseline over the burned area. I screamed in agony, and finally fainted from the pain, going to a dark place inside myself for relief.

The next morning, the wool blanket placed over me as I slept had glued itself to the Vaseline. The pain was too great to remove it myself. My mother tried to gently pull the blanket off the now bloody oozing burn, but there was no easy way to do it.. Finally, with an abrupt jerk, she simply yanked the blanket off. The wound, partially dried, began to ooze again. It would take weeks for the checkerboard wound to heal into a fully formed checkerboard scar.

My introduction to pain had been unforgettable. Little did I know our lifelong companionship had just begun.

*   *   *

I was born on the south side of Los Angeles in June 1960, with Sickle Cell Disease. Sickle cell disease is a heredity blood disorder, chronic and lifelong. It causes normal round blood cells to take on a sickle shape, blocking blood vessels and depriving the body of oxygen. Because of reduced blood circulation caused by sickle cell disease, wounds take longer to heal. Sickle cell disease was the reason my painful burn from the floor heater would not heal. It was also the reason my sister Cynthia died just months before I was born.

The story I was told about how Cynthia died was that she was diagnosed with sickle cell disease early in life. I was told my mother often visited the free-clinic with Cynthia, who was always being treated for one illness or another. At the time, my family was split—some kids going to church with my father, others staying home with my mother. Cynthia happily went to church and received my father's loyalty and blessing. Cynthia was popular and beautiful, and while at church she caught the eye of one particular young man. Soon, she became very pregnant.

At seventeen and still in high school, Cynthia married the young man. Not long after the celebration,

Cynthia started having problems with the pregnancy. Doctors diagnosed severe anemia and authorized a blood transfusion. Her teenage husband didn't know what to do, so he reached out to my father for help. He and my father worked together to figure out what to do and that's when Cynthia's real troubles began.

My father, a short man with a bad attitude, ran his house like a drill sergeant and showed love with his fist. To keep him happy my sisters and brothers had to show him loyalty. This meant going to his church, standing with him against my mother, or doing whatever he said. In this environment, everyone lived in fear.

When my sister got sick, my father, a Jehovah's Witness, would not allow her to get a blood transfusion.

Jehovah's Witnesses are known for their door-to-door preaching. Their belief system differs from traditional Christian theology and demands its members maintain unquestioning obedience. At the time, his church's belief was that people should not drink blood—and receiving a blood transfusion, by a doctor, in a hospital, was considered drinking blood. As irrational as that seems, accepting a blood transfusion for any reason was grounds for expulsion from the church. My father and his fellow church members believed in obeying the word of God at all cost.

My mother was not a "good" Jehovah's Witness, and didn't believe what my father did. She was a frail woman who had one baby after another for almost fifteen years. Her face was still beautiful, but her body was worn down. The family fighting had reduced her to an empty shell. She hadn't felt loved since the first day of her marriage. And the nuns from the local church who visited our home, bearing food, clothes and comfort for her many children, convinced her divorce was not an option.

Already overwhelmed by our family's poverty, and my father's abuse, when Cynthia's medical crisis arrived, my mother had no leverage. She felt powerless and had the entire Jehovah's Witness church against her. My older sisters and brothers all took sides. Either they were for the church, and my father, or against the church and therefore God.

Cynthia was miscarrying, losing too much blood and losing the baby. She needed a transfusion, and doctors needed her teenaged husband and my father to agree. Both being good Jehovah's Witnesses, both disagreed. The doctor's secretly tried to administer a blood transfusion anyway. My father literally blocked the door. Her doctor then sought a court order to administer the much-needed blood to my sister. But the judge, a stickler for respecting religious beliefs, denied the action.

My mother begged Cynthia to agree to receive the transfusion. Even in the last hours of life, Cynthia remained loyal to our father. A few hours later, with a low red-blood cell count, her body began to die, causing a full-blown sickle cell crisis. She died at the age of seventeen, six months pregnant with her unborn child.

My mother, who at the time was six months pregnant with me, internalized her pain and lashed out hatred toward everyone. She never forgave my father or the Jehovah Witness church. Not knowing she also carried a sickle cell disease gene, she blamed him for giving the disease to their children. One year later, when I was one years-old, while my mother was pregnant with my younger sister Kelly, my parents finally divorced.

Battle lines were now formally drawn. The family was torn apart, with the some older children living with my father and the others with my mother. For the first year of my life, I didn't know my father and never missed him when he left. My parents' divorce was just a formality. Our home was always divided and this was all I ever knew.

2
THE INTERNAL BOMB

After my wonderful fourth birthday, we moved from the house with the heater smack in the middle of the living room floor to a bigger house on the west-side of Los Angeles called mid-town. The neighborhood was full of middle-class, educated African-American families. This was in stark contrast to my mother: a poor, single woman on welfare, with a bunch of teenagers and dirty younger kids of all ages. We stood out like a stain in their clean environment.

So did our house. It was old, smelly and in great need of repair, its façade a strange light blue color. Its present condition was almost ludicrous: the once-elegant residence had two balconies, two kitchens, and what had once been a maid's quarters. There was even a secret closet flush to the wall. When closed it did something magical: it disappeared.

I loved the mysteriousness of that big old house. As one of the youngest kids, not yet in school, I could spend my days exploring all its nooks and crannies. But it was that secret closet that gave me a gift I would use for the rest of my life.

One day Ross, one of my older brothers who lived with my father, was visiting. He called me over to the secret closet and told me to look inside for a surprise. I did, looking forward to a new adventure. I went in and the door shut behind me.

Trapped inside, I realized there was no door knob, nor light. I couldn't recognize any of the objects I felt surrounding me. Suddenly, I was terrified. I cried and hit the walls, but no one heard me. Now it wasn't only the outline of the door that was invisible. I was too.

Finally tired of crying, I slid down the wall and crouched in the corner. As hours passed, I sank slowly into a place I didn't know yet. A place I would come to know very well: the quiet place inside myself.

That day, the place I found inside myself is where I went to gain peace from my fear. This was, I realized, the same place I'd gone when I'd burned my leg. It was also the place of refuge I found when I suffered many times with untreated pain and had been left alone in the night, crying and calling out for my mother. Now, I was there again to simply, quietly endure. My body couldn't escape the horror of being trapped in this closet. But I could escape it in my mind.

Hours later, I was awakened by someone carrying me out. It was late at night, and I was sent straight to bed. The next day Ross was gone and I never got a chance to talk to him about what he had done. Soon after he was shipped off to the military, I didn't see him again until years later. Ross never knew by trapping me in that closet he gave me a gift to last my entire life. The gift of quiet endurance would help me bear the life that was ahead of me.

Shortly thereafter, I became aware of a ticking bomb inside my body.

I was always a sickly child, skinnier than most kids, always with a cold or flu. This didn't stop me however from running and playing with kids in my neighborhood. I'd play all day and sometimes into the night: kicking balls, climbing trees, and fighting with my sisters Kelly and Macy.

We were labeled "the poor kids" in our neighborhood, but I didn't care. Some of my friend's parents were kind and overlooked my obvious poverty. Others would gawk and not let their kids play with me. I didn't care about that either. I was an inquisitive kid, who just so happened to also be poor, black, and with some strange soreness throbbing deep in my bones. I knew I was different.

10

During the night, I would tell my mother I felt pounding in my legs or arms and she'd tell me to ignore it. I couldn't ignore it. The pain was constant and all I could do was weep. I didn't know what was happening to me. None of my other sisters and brothers suffered with any sort of pain and I didn't understand what was happening to me. They helplessly watched as I suffered all day and in to the night. Sickle cell disease was showing itself alive in my body.

When I was six, one night, I had a sickle cell crisis. I didn't know what was happening to me but somehow the pain felt more intense. This kind of pain demanded more than tears. All I could do was rock back and forth, and moan.

A sickle cell crisis is when your body's red blood cells change shape from round to a sickle shape. The sickle shaped blood gets blocked in your veins and limits circulation to your body. At six, I didn't understand any of this. Even though my mother had one child die from the affects of a sickle cell crisis, she didn't understand either.

One day, after many nights of suffering, my mother bought a vibrating object that looked like an iron. It had round peg legs, and was covered with blue rubber and as heavy as a 10-pound dumbbell weight. Once the iron was plugged in, it buzzed and shook wildly. My mother pressed it to my arms and legs, assuring me it would "shake the blood loose." But it only shook the pain deeper into my bones.

I remember some dark nights, when I cried in pain, my mother would tell me to be quiet and stand over my bed, barking, "Your father gave you this problem!" Other nights, she'd laugh at me and joke, "The sickles are sickling again!" I didn't know what that meant, and I couldn't understand how she could be so cold. What I didn't know as a child is that my mother's hate for my father turned into disgust for her children.

I came to understand, without her help, that I had to pay attention to my pain, and become tougher to endure it. When it hurt, I would hurt along with it— and I would have to find ways to comfort the pain on my own. I'd rub my arms and legs, then go to my internal place of peace and patiently wait for relief.

Summer camp was another relief from the many pains in my life. Each year, the Salvation Army sponsored a trip for inner-city kids to spend one week in the country. My younger sister Kelly, older sister Macy and I always went. That year, we were sent to a camp run by a Catholic church and managed by nuns. It was high in the mountains and seemed to offer new adventures for all of us. I was so excited. I loved going to camp; it was my escape from reality, a place to meet new friends and have new adventures outside of my miserable home.

Our arrival started as usual—we each packed one suitcase of shorts and t-shirts and were driven to the bus pick-up point at church. When we arrived, children were already lined up to board the buses. I jumped out of our still-running car without even saying goodbye to my mother, and ran towards the person holding a clipboard.

On the bus ride to camp we passed tree-lined winding roads and flowing rivers. I watched outside the window as the sun peeked over mountain tops and we climbed up toward heaven. I felt the weight of the world lift from my young shoulders and flow out of the window into the wilderness. I felt the joy of my fourth birthday again, and the peace of my inner place. I felt happy again.

When we pulled up to the camp grounds, the first thing we did was drop off our suitcases and go to the mess hall for lunch. This room smelled of ham, turkey, mashed potatoes, green beans, and hot rolls. The only time I'd ever seen food like that was on Thanksgiving, when a church or food bank would give our family a turkey with all the trimmings. To me, this regular lunch was a banquet.

But after lunch, when we returned to our bunks to unpack, I promptly threw up the delicious lunch. I lay down on my bunk bed, where I threw up again. I couldn't stop vomiting. Soon I began to get the chills, and then I blacked out. I found out later the staff

13

carried me to the nurse, who watched me get worse for two hours. Finally, she called my mother.

I don't remember being carried to my mother's waiting car, or the long drive home, or being put in Macy's bed. I only woke up the next day to my mother putting an ice tray on my naked chest. It was so cold it felt hot, and I screamed. Removing the tray, my mother looked down at me in disgust. She told me she'd had to rent a car to drive me home. Unfortunately, the money she'd spent seemed to be her focus instead of my near death experience.

That experience was my introduction to the effects of high altitude on people with sickle cell disease. As I found out later, because oxygen at higher altitudes is thinner, my body could not get enough oxygen to function normally. Also, without oxygen, my red blood cells began to die at a higher rate. Luckily, I hadn't sustained serious damage to my internal organs or needed a blood transfusion. The nurse had known enough to call my mother and get me to a lower altitude quickly.

After this summer camp event, I started to realize I needed to have a short memory. To endure the painful episodes of my life, I had to forget how badly my mother treated me. I had to ignore the physical pain I felt on a daily basis, and endure her emotional and physical abuse too. I was learning an important lesson.

3
BEING DIFFERENT

My father's abandonment kept the family on welfare until my mother married our new stepfather, a cheerful man who was 20 years younger than she. Needless to say, their union was odd. I'd just turned five years-old and it had only been four years since her divorce from my father.

Although my mother was still quite beautiful, she had thirteen children and now a husband in his early twenties. He seemed to love her deeply, and made her smile so that part made sense. It was, however, more than my older brothers and sisters could tolerate. The boys left home to be with my father, who had moved around quite a bit since the divorce. And, as always, those children who embraced his religion were accepted. The others had to fend for themselves.

A few months later we welcomed a new baby sister, Grace. Grace was a beautiful brown baby, with soft black curly hair. She was darker-skinned than the rest of us, which seemed to make my mother overly protective. We were barely able to touch her without my mother shooing us away. But my mother, for once, was happy. I was glad to see her smile.

As the baby grew, and my older sisters began to mature, my mother felt a new threat. Her young husband began to behave like a father a little too strongly. The older girls scattered: two to live with an aunt in Michigan, one to an early marriage, and one to a Catholic boarding school run by nuns. Eventually, they were all gone, leaving only Grace, Kelly, Macy, Barbara and me behind. As the family size decreased, we moved across the street to a smaller less tacky house. Our sophisticated neighbors viewed it all.

Though my new stepfather worked all the time and went to school at night, he made up for his time away by being kind and gentle. Weekends, we'd pack up the station wagon and he'd take us to a friend's ranch in the country to ride horses and swim. They didn't mind us kids climbing in their trees, running through their fields and daydreaming while floating in their pool. My mother and stepfather even bought two horses, she a beautiful brown stallion and he a gallant Appaloosa.

While everyone else rode horses, I'd stay in the swimming pool until my fingers and toes were wrinkled and numb. I'd lie looking at the billowing

16

clouds form into elephants, or people's faces. I'd imagine God was playing with me, showing me new and different images with each gust of wind. It was a break for me from the physical pain I endured most of the time. In the real world, I couldn't run fast or jump high—I was weak all over. When we played ball, I was always the worst on my team. But in the pool, my body was flexible and no longer my enemy.

But five years of marriage wore my young stepfather down. The financial and emotional burden of another man's children was simply too much for him to bear. Shortly after I turned ten, my mother and stepfather started to fight bitterly and often. He began staying away from home for days at a time, and finally moved out. And after a second divorce, my mother once again was scared, alone, and left with a house full of children looking to her to make sense of what was happening.

To ease the financial strain, my mother immediately rented out our garage to a family of Native Americans. Mr. and Mrs. Bear—just like the nursery rhyme—had recently left the Indian reservation for Mr. Bear to take a job in the city. Mrs. Bear stayed home with their children, a baby, and Tommy, their young son, who was about my age. They all had round faces with light brown skin, dark eyes and straight black hair, and I couldn't stop watching them.

Unlike our newly separated family, the Bear Family, I soon noticed, seemed to laugh and play together. Our

17

home never had laughter. They were a family who seemed to cling to each other. While Mrs. Bear was kind to our family, she kept her distance. Mr. Bear seemed to work all the time. Every day, I'd see him leave early with his lunch pail, walking with his head down toward the car.

Our backyard was their front yard, and at first, whenever they cooked, I'd sit outside and inhale the rich smells. One day, Tommy came outside and noticed me looking into his house. He had rejected my attempts to be friendly, but I still wanted to know him. Because he didn't go to school with us, I had no idea what he did during the day. I was determined to get to know this kid and was relentless in my pursuit of him. My efforts eventually paid off when he began to play with me and my sisters. However, playing with him meant being bullied while he laughed and pushed us around.

Sometimes, I'd come home and see him sitting in the yard staring into space, looking sad. He'd see me looking and suddenly turn angry. Looking back, I can see he must have been terrified living in this new place, with no connection to anyone who looked like him or his family.

In the meantime, to make more money to pay the rent, my family doubled-up together and shared bedrooms. My mother rented our spare bedrooms to a student from Africa, and a husband and wife from Honduras. I was fascinated by the couple from

18

Honduras. They had dark black skin, but spoke Spanish. The wife wore colorful dresses and a head scarf and danced around and sang while cooking on a hot plate in their room. She let us kids sample whatever she cooked: spiced chicken, rice and beans, fried bananas and yams. I sat at her feet as she told stories about her country. While listening, I'd try to envision the wonderful trees and mountains she described, barely able to imagine how beautiful they must have been. I daydreamed about their lives, what it would be like to live in their countries.

I hadn't yet experienced hate or discrimination, so I only enjoyed experiencing what made them different and special. I loved our new roommate's food, dress and language; I loved that they were so foreign from mine. I also loved our Native American tenants too. The beauty of their Indian faces. So beautiful and different..

Within my limited experience, I was already living with the being different. For me, being different caused pain, so I had to hide it. I couldn't control what happened in my body, but I could control how I was going to respond to it. I saw my new neighbors, who couldn't control their differences, embrace them. Beautiful black skin, colorful languages, wonderful food and music. I soaked it all in.

It was far more difficult to figure out how to embrace being poor, something I didn't realize I was until I saw people who weren't. My neighborhood friends had furniture that actually matched, table lamps with shades. As simple a thing as a full refrigerator divided us. It's only when you see people eating you notice you haven't had a meal in a while.

My friend Margo lived in one of those well-kept homes, everything in perfect order. The living room was positively formal, with its find drapery and crystal vases just waiting for me to break them by accident. In Margo's house, I was extra-careful. Everything sparkled, and for the first time I understood how poor I was. And though her mother was well-off, she still worked. She had remodeled their garage into a day care center, and every day, the working professionals of the neighborhood dropped their crying babies off with her. Whenever I'd visit Margo, her mom would be barking orders to her employees or running after an unruly child.

She also was consistently kind to me. A pot of beans and rice was always boiling in her kitchen, and I would inhale the spices as if they alone could feed me. Margo tried to interest me to play with her new Barbie dolls, but I was only interested in a bowl of beans and rice. Margo's mother must have eventually noticed how skinny I was, and she began to pull me into her kitchen, where she'd sit me at the long table and feed me along with the babies, who were so well-fed they threw their food or ignored it completely.

But when Margo's father came home, he would see me eating with the children and look at me in disgust.

So did many of my other friends' parents, who'd call their kids inside when they saw me playing in their yards. To them, I was a dirty street kid. I tried not to let it hurt my feelings. After all, only the parents focused on my poverty. My friends who lived in those large, well-manicured homes—they never noticed.

What *was* hard for me to see was that my friends had food, toys, and they had love. My family consisted of fourteen kids, none of us was close to the other. My older brothers and sisters came and went, and we younger ones mimicked our parents, knowing how to fight and abuse each other but not how to care for and love one another. My friends asked, "Why did your parents have so many children?" I had no answer. It certainly wasn't because of love.

Even with a house full of tenants, after a year, my mother realized she couldn't afford the rent on this big ole house. The life she tried to manage without a husband became too much for her to bare.

Somehow, my mother convinced my father to let us stay with him until she got on her feet. Keeping Grace with her, she put Macy, Kelly, and I on a Greyhound bus. We were going to travel 500 miles, to Northern California, to live with a man we didn't even know.

4
500 MILES

Macy, Kelly and I, at twelve, ten and eleven years-old, like three dirty little amigos were going from Los Angeles to San Jose on a Greyhound bus. Barbara, at fifteen, was sent to my father's house weeks ahead of us. Being a light-skinned, blond-haired introvert, Barbara was tortured by our black neighbors and happily left as soon as she could. Before sending us to my father, my mother had given me a haircut like a boy. I was horrified she had cut off my long wavy braids and was sending me to his house with a short curly afro.

Though it was only 500 miles, it might as well have been across the country. We'd never been anywhere before. My mother didn't kiss us or tell us to be safe—one minute we were in the car, and the next she was leading us up the bus stairs to plunk us in the front row. "Sit near the driver and stay on the bus!"

were her parting words, and she didn't look back. As we pulled away from the station, no one said a word.

The shock of how my mother sent us away quickly turned to awe. Where I came from, cement covered every exposed piece of earth.

The small farm where my mother and stepfather had kept horses couldn't compare to the sights that passed my window. Land with nothing on it except rolling hills covered with dry grass, and odd-looking oak trees shaped like people making poses passed before me. I hadn't known there were farms full of cows, or rows of trees as far as the eye could see. We drove through small towns, farmlands, long empty roads. As we travelled to northern California, we passed farm workers going up and down the endless rows of onions in the broiling sun. We passed a sign advertising grapes and California raisins. Until that minute, I hadn't realized raisins were made from dried grapes.

I also studied the passengers coming on and off the bus, their clothes and hats and shoes. I imagined where they were going, where they had been. As the bus driver called each stop, I decided that his job— taking people to different places—was one of the most important you could have. I was fascinated by it all.

After one full day on the road, my father met us at the bus station, led us toward his used station wagon, and put our luggage in car. He didn't know us and we didn't know him. We drove to his home in silence.

But that was the least awkward part of our meeting. The last time my father lived in our household I was one years-old, when my parents divorced. But although I was meeting him for the second time in my life, it was his wife I couldn't take my eyes off of. When we entered the house his wife met us at the door. Her name was Cindy, and she was white. I'd lived in a black neighborhood my whole life and I'd never even talked to a white person, except for teachers at school. Now, my first real conversation with a white person would be with my new stepmother.

When my father introduced Cindy, a middle-aged German looking woman, she smiled with a large gap between her front teeth. I smiled back, thinking of my mother's beautiful round face. Looking through large rimmed glasses, her blue eyes scanned over us. "Hello girls," she said. "What grades are you in?" I looked over her stout body frame and answered blankly, being more consumed with looking around my new environment.

Also meeting us that day were Barbara and our new stepsisters, Paula and Janice. Barbara stood silently in the background as Cindy introduced her teenage daughters from a previous marriage.

I'd never seen real hippies before, but my stepsisters were typical 1960s California girls: bare feet, low-slung jeans, love beads, long hair, and lots of dark eye makeup.

Paula, the oldest, was already in high school. She had large gaps between her teeth and was very pale, just a little too skinny to be attractive. She'd dyed her hair black, and it hung down over her eyes. Though she greeted us politely, I could tell right away she wasn't at all interested in hanging out with four dirty black kids from Los Angeles.

Janice was fourteen and still in middle school—she was not much older than Macy—and was bubbly and excited to meet us. When she smiled, you could see her straight white teeth, and her eyes sparkled. She was beautiful. With her blond, flowing hair she looked just like my friend Margo's Barbie doll. She also looked like her mother, give or take 30 years.

But we learned right away that our stepsisters' casual dress was the only carefree part of my father's household. As Janice showed me the house and my bedroom, she told me the house rules: dinner at 6:00 p.m., and church not only Sunday, but Wednesday and Saturday too.

My father and his new wife were apparently very much practicing Jehovah's Witnesses. In just one day, after 500 miles, my whole life had changed. I had been free to run the streets, eating whatever I could get my hands on. Now, faced with dinner at 6 and weekly churchgoing this was going to take some getting used to.

At our first dinner together, I realized how nice it was to have a hot meal waiting. My three sisters and I were so unused to dining at a table that we spilled food all over the tablecloth. And the next day, as the family prepared to set off for church, we ate a hot breakfast, something I'd never had at my mother's. At eleven years-old, this was a happy change from my usual breakfast of donuts and coffee.

My sisters and I immediately realized we hadn't bought any clothes fit for church. We didn't even own any dresses. My father told Janice to give each of us one of her skirts. They were long and ugly, with wide straight hems at the ankle. I didn't want to be caught dead in one of those Quaker looking multi-colored skirts. My hair was bad enough. "I don't wear long skirts," I told her, hoping that would get me off. My father overheard and was not amused. "Put it on," he said coldly. My brothers and sisters had told me of his famous beatings. I quickly obeyed.

The church was another surprise. It was a mixed-race congregation, whites and blacks all mingling and talking to one another. The other parishioners greeted us kindly, though they seemed a little too nice. I could just imagine what they'd been told about my sisters and me before we got there. I had heard so many scary stories from my mother about Jehovah's

26

Witnesses, I was afraid that someone was going to try to capture my soul, if such a thing was even possible. But we sat in our row, surrounded by singing and clapping. From how they interacted and worshiped, it seemed unlikely that they were evil, as my mother had insisted. They were just a group of people who strongly believed their faith, whether right or wrong.

The elementary school my father enrolled us in was the brainchild of a progressive school board that had decided to integrate hearing and deaf children. I had never known a deaf person or seen sign language before, and I was immediately intrigued by my new classmates, gesturing and speaking soundlessly with each other.

But the students would have to go beyond deaf and hearing to categorize me. My favorite singing group was the Jackson 5, and Michael Jackson was my idol. For my first day, I had dressed in my favorite bell-bottoms, sporting a wide-collared colorful shirt and new short-cut afro, which I had finally figured out how to style. As my stepmother signed the admission papers, everyone in the office gawked, and as we walked through the halls to my new classroom, students and teachers alike literally stopped in their tracks.

My first teacher made no effort to put me at ease. Placing me smack in the front of the class, he barely let me take my seat before asking me the capitol of Luxembourg. I had no clue. I had only attended a black inner-city public school that barely had books, let alone geography classes. I looked at my new white classmates for help, but they all looked away. There was nothing else to do. I looked back at him and replied, "I don't know." Everyone laughed, including the teacher. Almost gleefully, he informed me, "The capitol of Luxembourg is Luxembourg!"

From that moment, I hated him, his comb-over hair and front tooth that stuck out over his lip. I would never be laughed at for my ignorance again, I decided. In this new place, I would study hard and know as much as anybody else.

My first real friend at that school was deaf. I met her on that first day when, at lunchtime, I approached some of the deaf kids sitting on the playground, where they sat gathered with their heads pulled together. I had to wave to get their attention. "What are you guys doing?" I asked. They all looked away. Suddenly, I felt ridiculous with my afro and multicolor shirt. I waved my hands again, asking them the question I'm sure I wanted to ask myself: "WHY ARE YOU AT THIS SCHOOL?"

That broke the ice. They looked at each other and made laughing faces. They touched my hair, which must have been strange to them—pointing to my clothes, lip-reading each other's mouthings. Then, suddenly, we were all laughing with each other—they at my curious clothes, me at how bizarre it was to speak without sounds.

28

My new friend taught me how to move my fingers to say "Hi," and every day, I would walk past the deaf kids and sign hello. They loved it. And I loved having new friends to play with, and a secret language the "talking kids" didn't know. I was used to feeling different. But this made me feel different, special, and accepted. I liked it.

I'm sure it made the deaf kids feel special too, because talking kids usually didn't socialize with them. If the hearing kids even noticed them at all, they'd only walk by, push them out of the way or make fun of their muted sounds. In that school, it was a big deal to have a talking kid want to learn sign language. I was happy to be the first.

As the year drew on, I became one of the most popular people in the school. It wasn't because I tried to fit in. It was because I was a natural rebel. Not only did I look and dress different, I was the only hearing kid who was unafraid to be friends with the deaf kids. Because I wasn't ashamed, eventually, the hearing kids decided that it was cool to do sign language and they wanted to learn. It grew so that at lunch time, hearing kids surrounded the deaf kids and me and watched as we spoke with our hands. Yes, I was the school's first black person. But I had integrated it in more than one way.

5
CAN YOU SAY 'FIGHT'?

Just before I graduated from elementary school, one of my hearing friends, Julie, asked me to come over to her house after school. The rules of Jehovah's Witnesses left little room for socializing, so it was a treat to visit my friend. Julie was a hippy-in-training, and though her all-white neighborhood was only a few blocks away, its pristine houses, where flowers grew in every yard, might as well have been miles from my home. My home always had a junk truck my father used for his part-time junk business parked in the driveway.

Julie thought my personality was wild and colorful, and so did her older sister Silvia, who, as a full-blown hippy, proud of her "radical" little sister for having a black friend. She smiled when she saw me in their kitchen. But when Julie took me into the living room to introduce me to her mother, the elegant woman looked me up and down; her face frowned below her perfectly teased bird's nest hair.

"You can't have company right now," she told Julie, with a harsh tone.

By then, I was no longer shocked by casual racism. I'd seen it before. When I was treated badly, I no longer felt ashamed. In this case, I felt bad for Julie's mother. I had known exactly how those deaf kids felt, ignored and abused. How they didn't have a choice to be born deaf. How it wasn't *their* fault. Julie's mother saw my difference and couldn't embrace it. It was her loss. I overlooked her ignorance and remained friends with Julie anyway.

I spent the summer exploring San Jose with Janice and my sisters. By then, Paula had moved in with her Mexican boyfriend, Barbara stayed in her room, as usual. My father worked two jobs and never knew of our escapades. Cindy was happy Janice kept us out of the house.

Janice took Macy, Kelly and me around town, where we'd walk barefoot and thumb rides with strangers. Then, no one wanted to be a stranger to anyone else. Everyone called each other brother and sister, even people they'd never met. Hippies with flowing skirts and flowers in their hair danced anywhere and everywhere. Janice introduced us to Black Panthers, Christians, Jews—people of all races. In my child's eyes, they lived lives without walls, without prejudice. That was my plan, too.

During that time, the mood of northern California in the 1970s began to change. Julie's mother was becoming outdated, with everyone, it seemed, interested in embracing difference—literally. On the streets, I saw black men with white women, white men with black women, and their beautiful mixed brown babies everywhere. As junior high approached, it was becoming the height of the Black Pride movement. With hair now grown into a full-blown afro, I happily agreed with the concept.

But junior high threw a quick wrench into my plans. In my new school, the hippie creed of peace, love and happiness had been passed over for gang rule, with Mexican students and white students fighting openly. Black Pride was unheard of, with Macy and I being the only black kids. By now, I was unafraid to be different, but unprepared for what was to come. All of my white friends had gone to a better school across town, while my deaf friends had been sent to a special school. My sister and I were once again completely on our own.

When the Mexicans and whites weren't fighting with each other, they kept to different sides of the campus. I pretended to be tough, never looking directly at anyone. I knew Macy and I would be made to choose, and of course, they tested us immediately.

It was a scrawny white girl with stringy hair who first stepped in front of me to pick a fight. Motivated by her gang, she confidently pressed toward me. I wasn't afraid. Being born in inner-city Los Angeles, of course I knew how to fight. But my time in northern California had changed me. Before, I would have felt the need to prove myself. Now, I knew she was only trying to prove how tough she was by fighting me, and I pitied her. I stepped aside and continued on my way.

Of course, that wasn't the end of it. It was hard for anyone to provoke me directly on school grounds, but the bullies weren't safe when they followed me and Macy home, taunting us, shouting names like "nigger" and "blackie" at our backs. The Mexican gang was close behind, watching to see what would happen with the white gang. We kept walking, until the girl jumped in front of me, blocking my path. I stepped around her, and she grabbed my shoulder, throwing me forward. I stopped, turned around and socked her right in the jaw. Before I knew it, I was on top of her, beating her right in the face. The white gang girls kept trying to pull me off, while the Mexican gang held them back, yelling, "Fair fight!"

The fight became so violent that we moved like one body down the street, both gangs following and cheering. Still, I felt oddly removed from what was going on. I watched their cheering faces as if I was a ghost, wondering what they were cheering about. And even as I punched and kicked the girl, I wondered with frustration why she'd pushed me into the fight in the first place.

Finally, a passerby threatened to call the police. Someone pulled me off the girl. The gangs scattered. My sister, who'd done nothing to help me, walked home with me in silence. I wondered, "What had hurt the girl so badly that beating me up would have made it better?"

When I woke up the next morning, I didn't have a mark on me. At school, the girl on the other hand, was deeply bruised, her faced covered in scrapes. Taken aback by her injuries, I reminded myself that she had been asking for it. The fight, ironically, had turned me into a kind of superstar: kids I didn't even know saying hi to me and patting me on the back, laughing to each other about how badly I had beaten that girl. I wasn't at all proud of the fight. In fact, the only way I could overcome my guilt was by reminding myself that I had to do it to protect myself and my sister.

At lunch, the head girl of the Mexican gang, with eyes lined in heavy black liner, rings on every finger and long black teased hair, congratulated me for standing up for myself. She said they were going to protect me from the white gang from now on. "The black girls," she told me, "were not to be touched." And we weren't. The fight cemented me and my sister's position in school. I was tired of playing tough, and I appreciated any break from it.

At home, things had also begun to fray at the edges. Cindy and my father had just had another baby, and Cindy began suffering with what we now know as post-partum depression. Then, none of us knew why she'd cry for no reason, or hear household objects speaking to her. I stayed out of her way, and Paula stopped coming home to visit. Even Janice began keeping away from the house.

My father, though his wife was in crisis, never asked any of us, "How was your day?" or "How are you doing?" Though we lived in the same house, we all dealt with our issues separately. I was avoiding conflict with two gangs, Barbara avoided everything by staying in her room, Kelly was terrified most times, and Macy was becoming very angry. My father left us to all deal with it alone, disengaged from any semblance of a family. He went to work; we went to school, to church and then straight to our rooms.

I began to rebel against that sterile, cold environment. Cindy had always bossed us around when my father wasn't home, but now, I began to rebel against her just for fun. One day, at breakfast I refused to read their Jehovah Witness' book of daily devotions. Cindy' face turned red, she picked up the book and threw it right in my face. I stood up from the table, facing Cindy in defiance, then left the house immediately. I wanted Cindy to know I wouldn't be pushed around anymore, but I was still terrified she'd tell my father what I'd done. But she must have been afraid of the repercussions too. Cindy kept this event to herself, I never heard another word about it.

Between the school gangs and my father's dysfunctional home, I began to long to go back to my mother in Los Angeles. Life there was difficult, but at least my mother wasn't a stranger to me. It turned out to be easier than I'd thought to get there. I simply went to school one day and walked into the principal's office. I announced I didn't want to go home to my father's house anymore, and neither did Macy. "Our father makes us go to church too much," I told the principal. It was hardly child abuse, but to get the matter off her plate, the principal called Child Welfare Services and turned us over to a social worker.

Our father didn't object—he never called us or asked us to change our minds. In fact, he didn't contact us at all. We found ourselves shipped off to juvenile hall, a kind of kid's jail, where we spent three long days. On the third day, we found out they had arranged for Macy, Kelly and me to be flown back to our mother in Los Angeles. Barbara decided to stay in San Jose where she fit in better. No one was at the airport to wave goodbye except the social worker we didn't know.

This was the first time I'd seen an airplane close-up. And, it was going to be my first flight. Not dwelling on the fact that I'd spent two years with a father whom I still didn't know, I was once again distracted by the adventure ahead of me. Watching the mountains, clouds and stewardess' faces, I was glad I made the decision to leave my father and his church. A few hours later, we landed in Los Angeles, and stepped off the plane into my mother's angry arms.

6
KING DREW

While we were away living with my father in San Jose, my mother moved to a small two bedroom apartment in a very bad neighborhood in South Los Angeles. Coined "South-central" by local police, it was one filled with poor angry people and their wild children.

It was a place of poverty and despair, where, if you were lucky, you'd avoid being shot, stabbed or overdosing on some illegal drug. It was a place people drove past, but never stopped.

The people who lived here feared for their lives and the lives of their children. Too afraid and overworked to fight back, drugs, gangs, and crime ruled. In this neighborhood, you closed your mouth and stayed alive. And your kids merely survived.

This neighborhood was very different from that black middle-class haven I expected to go back to. Our two bedroom apartment was also very different from the mildew mansion I expected to live in. They both added to my already long list of things to endure.

My mother, bitter and unfulfilled, consumed with the only child she appeared to love, by the only man who appeared to love her, had completely withdrawn from us. The abuse, poverty, hate and regret she endured made her withdraw from all acts of kindness.

My older siblings never came around to help ease our condition, so we toughened up quick. I didn't care that I was living with a bitter shell of a woman in a war zone. I was happy to be back in Los Angeles--and, though it was horrible, it was still better than going to church Monday, Wednesday, Saturday and Sunday.

Something else had changed since our time in San Jose. On our first day home, the neighborhood kids surrounded me and asked, "Who are you?" I told them plainly, "We just moved back with our mother after spending time with our father in Northern California." They laughed in my face. "You look like hippies, and you talk White!" they teased.

I couldn't believe it. At my father's, I had been the coolest Black kid in a hippy school—and now I was being called a White hippy. What were these kids talking about? I thought.

I decided to overlook their ignorance and play with them anyway. I had to figure out what this new environment was all about.

The next day my mother enrolled me and my sister's in school, leaving us without a hug or a piece of advice. It was now my second year of junior high, and here, I was smaller than everyone else, to say nothing of being a hippy-looking, light-skinned Black girl.

Talk about standing out. I had experience standing out. I knew how to get past it by being myself no matter what. I held my head up high and walked past their stares and gestures.

My first class was filled with Black and Asian kids, the latter of whom I'd never gone to school with before. I was interested in getting to know them, but soon learned there was an unwritten rule that Blacks and Asians didn't mix.

It was like having déjà vu. Like when the deaf kids and hearing kids who didn't mix, and the Whites and Mexicans. It was the separation of people I was forced to endure all over again.

Los Angeles had recently been torn apart by race riots, and my Black classmates dressed in militant outfits with big afros and bigger attitudes. That first day, they looked me up and down.

I wore my afro big too, but my clothes were different. I wore my usual homemade tie-dyed shirt and bell-bottom jeans, with make-up a little too dark.

The first question a Black kid asked me was, "What set are you from?" I had no idea what they were talking about. "What do you mean?" I said. When they discovered I had no clue, other's chimed in unison, "What *gang* are you with?"

In San Jose, I had already decided that gangs were for dummies and losers. But here, it seemed I might have to fight again.

"I'm not from any set," I said humbly.

They were stunned. "You talk White and you look White," someone said from the crowd. Again, I was struck by how hilarious it was to go from being the coolest, most popular Black kid in my school to a 'White-looking, White-talking' outcast in a Black school.

Being in the middle was nothing new for me, but I was tired of being defined, first by my race in San Jose, now by my skin color. Although I carry both black heritage and white heritage in my veins, I was raised Black.

Now, I was being forced between two worlds again; not black, not white. I felt like I had to come up with a new racial definition of myself just to be left alone. I sat there in my seat, between Asian kids and Black kids deciding to re-define who I was going to be.

Since the day the teacher made fun of me for not knowing the capital of Luxembourg, I had been a good student, always focused on doing well and learning. Again, I decided to get through my new school by concentrating on schoolwork, and ignoring gang affiliations. I decided to keep my head down staying out of everybody's way. I kept my eyes and ears open, looking at this new challenge and listening to both sides of the room.

I noticed immediately that teachers didn't push the Black students, or engage with us during class. Instead, they interacted with and encouraged the Asian students. The classrooms themselves seemed segregated, with the Asian students in front with the teachers, and the Black students in back, socializing. And, if a Black student—say, me—did well on an exam, they'd simply remind me of the school's cheating policy.

I'd been lucky to arrive in my new school close to summer break, when the gangs were focused on graduation and getting out of school, not fighting. And in my neighborhood, I purposely played with the younger kids, wanting to stay young myself as long as I could. Even the fact that our poverty ensured we lacked adequate food and clothing, that didn't keep me back—I managed to find odd jobs to stay afloat. But not every struggle was under my control.

During the entire time at my father's house, I had been in good health. I was used to always having an ache somewhere in my body, but I felt pretty good. I was getting proper food at proper mealtimes, and was forced to get rest by the fact that I couldn't run the streets. Sickle cell disease had been quietly watching, waiting for its chance to re-emerge.

At my mother's house, with no food, and no rest, Sickle cell would have no restrictions. I would often suffer with aching pain throughout my body, with fever, and soreness. For the first time, however, when it did re-emerge, I was able to get adequate health care.

Somewhere, my mother had found out about a new clinic in East Los Angeles that specialized in Sickle cell care. In the 1970s the American medical community got special funding to study patients with Sickle cell disease. Kelly, who also has the disease, and I were lucky enough to be included in this study. She had sickle cell too, but never had the complications I experienced.

The last physician I'd seen years earlier our "family" doctor, a seventy-five year old White man, who simply gave us kids vaccinations as needed. He never treated us for any of our Sickle cell related illnesses.

But this new clinic at King Drew Hospital was filled with young, Black doctors specializing in the treatment I'd desperately needed my entire life.

43

The hospital sponsoring the study sent a van to pick up patients every week. How we hated to see it come into our neighborhood! It had the hospital name, "King Drew," posted in big white letters across both doors, and our friends, walking to school would point and laugh at us as we were taken away. Though I hated to see that van coming, I loved to see my new doctors.

These physicians and their nurses greeted us with a smile. They didn't seem to see color or race. They simply saw people with a disease that the world ignored. They would take our blood, talk to us about our pain, and even explain what was causing it. Even though at the time, little was known about the disease, the medical staff explained that my blood disorder was caused by my red blood cells changing shape from round to sickle, and that the effects it had on my body were not *my* fault.

For the first time in my life, I could talk to someone about my pain and they understood. I had people to help me understand what was happening in my body, too. They were gentler with me than anyone had ever been, and, finally free of guilt that my "sickles were sickling," I could embrace my body with its faults and pains. I could finally embrace my difference.

The outside world was another story. Despite finding us a place to manage and monitor our disease, my mother still refused to discuss it beyond saying, "You got it from your father."

I often wondered if she was so traumatized by the death of my older sister, that she didn't want any connection to it. I also wondered if she took some of the blame for her death. Rather than become bitter about my mother's lack of concern, I often felt sorry for her life which was full of regrets.

My mother was a talented singer, but never got to express her gift. She was beautiful, posing in Jet magazine in 1953, but was beaten because men noticed. She was a dreamer, dreaming of a life rich and famous that would never materialize. And, she was bitter by what life could have been without my father.

Often times, my mother would brag, "I kept you kids together." As if she was doing us a favor. Then, she'd boast, "I could have left your father and you all would have been scattered." My mother was simply sharing her pain with us.

My neighborhood friends also didn't understand. While I worked odd jobs for small change, avoiding gangs at bus stops, I also thought it was time to notify my friends of my sickness.

"Why do you get sick all the time?" one friend asked. I answered proudly, "I have Sickle Cell Disease and I see special doctor's at that hospital that sends a van." My friend jumped away from me in horror. "Can I catch it?" she asked.

I knew enough about the disease to assure her that it was impossible, but after that, she not only avoided me, she told other neighborhood kids not to play with me, either.

After that, I vowed to never tell anyone I had Sickle Cell Disease again. I was determined to be "normal," and, if I got sick, I would tell my friends that I had a cold or flu. They didn't need to know the details of how in a sickle cell 'crisis' I would be in too much pain to move. They didn't need to know how my arms and legs would be swollen with veins blocked by sickled red blood cells.

If I was going to be judged or criticized for being different, I wasn't going to give out information to be used against me. I also kept secrets from myself.

In the 1970s, little was known about the long-term effects of Sickle Cell Disease. After I'd been part of the King Drew study for a while, during a routine exam, a misguided doctor told me, "You know, you probably won't live to be thirty years-old."

Because I was still young, this death sentence meant nothing to me. I wasn't even startled by the news. I thought, "Thirty years-old is a long time away!" I hid this secret in my memory and behaved like it was never said. Looking back, I cringe at that doctor's blunt, mis-guided delivered death sentence.

The study would end, and the van with the large white lettering would stop coming. Without my weekly visits, I realized that learning the truth about my disease wasn't all I had cared about. It was the kindness of those doctors and nurses that I'd never experienced before. And, besides the mis-guided death sentence, it was the knowledge they gave me that made those embarrassing trips in the van worthwhile.

7
ACTING 101

In my tough neighborhood, I always stayed one step ahead of getting beaten up, or drugged out. That summer, my mother, who was losing the last bit of control she had over us, mentally unplugged from the family. With her absent from reality, we ran wild. Macy ran away completely. Kelly stayed close to home with little Grace. I spent the whole summer playing in the streets and roaming from one friend's house to another. I needed to see what normal family life was like. I watched attentively as some of my friends' parents showed them love, imagining how good it must have felt. I promised myself that one day I would love and respect my children too.

I had one friend, Tonya, whose mother had a decent job and nicer apartment than most. Tonya's mother lavished her and her sister with clothes, shoes and hot cooked meals every day. She'd cook before going to work, leaving instructions to not feed "those" kids. Everyday, after she left, I'd go over to Tonya's and ask to look into her covered pots. She didn't see any harm in letting me look, but rarely offered to feed me. She knew I was hungry and ignored, felt sorry for me, but didn't take responsibility to share. She had developed her mother's selfish spirit.

I'd watch as Tonya paraded new clothes "Momma" had bought, hoping for a hand-me-down. No such luck. Tonya's mother showed love by buying whatever they wanted. And they got everything. She made sure they always had soda in the refrigerator and change in their pockets. In one way I hated Tonya. She had everything, I didn't. But in another way, I felt sorry for her. She didn't know how to survive, like I did.

The new school year brought more adult challenges. The previous year, I forced myself to be a child for as long as possible by playing in the streets like a kid. But over the summer, I grew into a young woman. I couldn't pretend to be a kid anymore. I had to get tough quick.

This year, I also didn't need any unwanted attention as the odd ball stand out. So, I read magazines to find out the latest clothes styles, and replaced my hippy clothes with thrift shop specials that looked new. I straightened my hair and experimented with different styles. I was ready.

The first day my homeroom was crazy, my fellow students yelling and throwing paper like confetti. I looked around and found a seat. I was determined to focus on school, no matter what happened. But that same old question cropped up again.

"What set are you from?" a classmate asked me, then another. I replied, "I'm not from any set." A girl pulled me aside. "You better get with a set," she said firmly. "Or you're going to get beat up!"

Macy had come back home and was now in senior high school, Kelly was with me in junior high. I wasn't scared of getting in a fight, but I knew Kelly was afraid of her own shadow and wouldn't fight back. I knew that I had to be strong for her, as well as for myself, because I knew if they beat me up, they were surely going to beat her up too. I got mad just thinking about how she wouldn't fight for herself, I resolved to find a "set" to protect us.

The girls in this school, like those in my neighborhood, were tough and didn't fight fair. They were known to use knives, razor blades, pens, pencils, and anything else with a sharp edge when they needed to. Using such weapons was against all of my beliefs, especially since I didn't want to fight in the first place. Still, I needed to survive. I decided the best solution was to create a gang member persona to scare off others before they could even threaten me.

But before I even had a chance, I was drawn into a fight. At a bus stop, while I was sitting waiting with other kids, a girl approached me with her gang. "You think you're pretty, don't you?" she said standing over me. I couldn't believe how stupid the question was. As I sat there pondering what to do, a classmate friend slipped a knife in my hand.

"If you need it, use it," she said. Not knowing what else to do, I quickly put the knife in my back pocket— just in time for the girl to grab me and push me off the bench.

I jumped into gear. Everything in me said "Fight back!" At first, I had the advantage, and I was on top, beating the girl's face. But she somehow pushed me over and started beating me. As the blows hit me again and again, a small internal voice said, "Take out the knife and use it!" Immediately another internal voice said, "Don't touch that knife or your life will be over!" Even as the girl beat me, I visualized myself outside the battle amazed by the sheer stupidity of it all.

Finally, I knocked the girl off of me and stood up. Just then, the bus arrived. Everyone except the girl I was fighting and her gang jumped in. I followed my friend and dropped down into my seat, exhausted. The girl who'd given me the knife patted me on the back. I couldn't speak. I was so angry that people would hurt each other for no reason at all. It was all senseless to me.

I understood being hurt, and being different. Being sick my whole life had taught me that life was hard enough without fighting. I gave the girl the knife back. I concluded she was no friend of mine.

That next day at school, I looked fine, but the girl I'd fought was badly bruised, no longer the big-talking leader of the pack. After our brawl, everyone at school was scared of me, as I'd wanted. I was glad, however, they didn't know about the knife. I was ashamed I'd even had it. I could sense that I'd earned that girl's respect, but nothing could have seemed more unimportant to me.

Still, the fight seemed to help me gain the reputation of a ruthless fighter. This fact also led to the respect of older girls in my neighborhood, who began to look out for me. They'd seen me the past summer on the street playing hopscotch or at the park, but now that I'd beaten the leader of another gang I was worthy of being a member of their group, and the youngest one. They called me their little sister, and I quickly got on board. I needed their friendship and protection. I watched them carefully: how they wore their hair, their clothes, and their makeup. To protect my own younger sister, I would have to learn to live in this neighborhood.

To complete my disguise, I started to hang out with the girl who was considered the toughest in our neighborhood. She was light-skinned black, like I was, long wavy hair and almost beautiful, except her face was very hard. When you looked deep into her eyes, you could see something had gone very wrong. She was broken.

This girl even the toughest girls were afraid of. But I chose her as my big sister, and for her own reasons, she chose me as her little one.

After school and weekends, I'd go to her house just to watch her. She was the toughest girl I had ever seen. I saw her beat up her boyfriend, order people around like servants, and jump over a fence in two leaps.

One time, I did something that got on her nerves. She drew her fist back and looked directly into my eyes. "Don't ever do that again!" she barked. I was scared to death of her. But I knew she was the key to my survival. I had to learn from her but never become like her.

I never really became a gang member, I just acted like one. Sure, I had the look: heavy makeup, straightened hair and boy clothes. And I also had the persona: talking tough, never being too friendly. Because I hung around the toughest female gang member in our neighborhood, people just thought I was one of them.

This new friendship led me back to my old street-kid ways. Although I ran the streets, I kept going to school and my grades never slipped. I imitated those tough girls but never became what they were—and they never noticed I was too smart to really join them.

Hanging around my new sister and her friends until all hours of the night, I avoided anything criminal. Even though my mother no longer influenced my actions, I knew I didn't want to see the inside of a jail.

My disguise had worked on both sides. I was a mystery to everyone, and my sister Kelly and I were safe. But Kelly wasn't so easy to fool. One day she came up to me at school, upset, and said, "My friend's say you're in a gang." I denied it.

She didn't know I had to become someone I wasn't in order to protect her. She would never experience being surrounded by a gang, or being beaten up. She had no idea she was able to go to school safely and have friends because of what I endured. And she would never know that because kids feared me, we were safe. Telling her would have ruined my act. Though I longed to tell her, I was just as scared as she was, I couldn't show it.

Ironically, the stress I was under also made me start to look at my mother and understand her struggles. How she mistreated my sisters and me reflected the mistreatment she felt herself. Her own family had abandoned her while she lived with my father in their abusive marriage. They offered no help and no way out.

Raising kids in poverty, with no car, she'd take buses late at night to odd jobs while we were free to run wild. When she'd come home our neighbors would immediately tell her about our activity in the neighborhood and how bad we were. Though she yelled at us, she had no control over me or Macy. Finally, she gave up.

At the time, I thought my mother was simply neglectful. But now I think that, like me, she was just trying to keep her sanity in a hopeless situation. My mother, sisters and I were all surviving the best way we could.

8
THE LOVE OF DANCE

Out of my seven living sisters, none have made an impact on my life, except one. My oldest sister Silvia was more like a distant mother, with no real connection to the realities of my life. I suffered and she, being married and with children of her own, had little involvement. The next one down, Yolanda, moved to Michigan when I was five years-old. She was raised by a distant aunt, and together they built a respectable life for her. Separate from the life I lived with my mother.

Yolanda wanted nothing to do with our family, and ignored all forms of acknowledgment of her past. She created a new identity, which did not include an abusive mother and father, or a bunch of poor sisters and brothers. She severed most ties with our family and lived a life worthy of her respectably created upbringing.

The next sister down was my older sister Kathy, who after my mother married my stepfather, was sent away to live with nuns. I don't know why she was sent away from home, but she would come back years later a cultured and educated woman.

Kathy had become the exception. She was quiet and gentle; like my own spirit yearned to be, and thoughtful, giving me a gift that would last my whole life.

One summer, Kathy came home to visit during a break from college. She studied dance at the University of California Los Angeles (UCLA). Kathy was six years older than me, and we had barely been raised together. So I really didn't know her.

When she came home to visit, I spent a lot of time just watching her, trying to figure her out. She was 6 feet tall and slender, with long legs, and graceful without trying to be. Wherever she stood her posture was erect, her head raised elegantly and body stood poised automatically. She had a pretty smile and warm eyes with ash blond hair. I'd never seen this sort of gentleness in my family before. She looked nothing like my mother.

While out of school, Kathy danced at home to keep in shape. To dance, she changed into skin-tight leotards, with leg warmers to the ankles and a headband neatly holding back her hair. She turned on the music and began to sway to the sound.

I discovered that in modern dance, each beat had a meaning; each change in tempo had a purpose. I watched as her arms followed the melody of the strings, they pulled her one direction after another. Her shoulders rolled back from the socket in perfect time. She seemed to let the music do the directing and her body followed its instruction.

Suddenly, she pulled one leg back and kicked it out, nearly touching the ceiling. I had never seen anything so beautiful. I had always loved music, but had never seen anyone move to each instrument. I was mesmerized by the control of her body. I, too, felt captive to the drums that seemed to move her.

I begged Kathy for a leotard and a pair of tights so I could try to move like her. She laughingly got a pair that obviously was too large for my 5'4" frame. The leotard hung on my body like rolls of excess skin, but I held it gathered, pretending it fit.

As sounds of blues infused trumpets poured out of the record player, it was as if I knew dance instinctively and it knew me. Dance poured out of my soul, and my body allowed my spirit to lead. Kathy watched as I twisted and turned, moving along with the notes. The music and my body communicated, sharing its sorrow and pain. I found a place where my body could speak, and discovered my story could be told with my body.

Kathy and I, almost strangers, had connected for the first time in our lives. I never knew what happened to her during her childhood. We never talked about it. Each child in my family suffered their own kind of agony. Some withdrew, some lashed out, while others quietly went about gathering pieces of a life and living it. Kathy did that. She went about gathering what the nuns taught her, and piecing together a life that now included dance. That summer, dance became part of my life as well.

After that, I was hooked. Dance had become to me a silent expression of what I was feeling inside. I strengthened my body with each contorted move. I went into my quiet place, while moving to music. It was a beautiful union.

As her little student, Kathy watched me. She would show me a graceful move and I'd try to imitate her gracefulness. She'd smile, show me again and I'd try harder to get the movement just right. As my mother was now a distant blur, I appreciated the time together with my long lost sister Kathy. We explored music and dance together, two of my new favorite things. Before returning to college, Kathy gave me that old leotard and a pair of tights.

After she left, I would turn on the radio to smooth jazz sounds and try to figure out what to do and how to do it. With sounds of soft trumpets and flutes blowing, I moved along with them. The movement cleared my mind of worries, leaving me both relaxed and powerful. My body tightened with every movement, strengthening every muscle needed to live my life of struggle.

Every chance I got, I escaped into the world of dance. Even dressed in a T-shirt and jeans, if I heard music, I'd sway, feeling myself flowing along. I immersed myself in reading biographies of great dancers like Alvin Ailey and Martha Graham. I studied their technique and style. I memorized their fingers and toes, the position of their neck. I studied the art of dance for its simple beautiful form.

As I progressed with my knowledge of dance movements, my living room had become too restrictive. I needed more room. I began going to the neighborhood recreation center gymnasium to test my moves on a bigger scale.

The Center had an employment program called "CETA" funded to employ disadvantaged youths for the summer. Local kids went to this Center to escape the streets, just as I went to dance to escape my pain.

After a manager at the Center saw me dancing in the gym, she hired me into the CETA work-program to teach dance to a class of about ten girls, ranging from age six to twelve. Not only did I have a new job, I had a job dancing. I took this new assignment very serious.

I wanted to look professional, so I pulled my hair back like dancers do, took off my heavy make-up, and wore the classic leotard and tights with a flowing skirt. My students couldn't afford leotards or tights, so I told them to just wear T-shirts, shorts and socks. It didn't matter that it looked like they were about to head off to play baseball. I wanted them to understand that clothes didn't limit us. In my classes, I showed these impoverished kids how the simple joy of dance freed us from everything, if only for an hour.

To hold class, first, I'd clear the basketball court of players. Then we'd line up along the bars bolted to the walls and stretch. The girls quickly learned that modern dance meant listening to your body. I told them to avoid moving quickly or erratically—to remain free, but stay in control. They understood instinctively. Smoothly they raised themselves on their sock-covered toes with great poise in imitation of ballerinas they'd seen on TV. They raised their arms, straightening their backs. "Stand up, chest out and shoulders back!" I encouraged. I knew they needed to stand up straight not only for dance, but for life, too.

Dance had given *me* a new life. Surrounded by poverty and hopelessness, I found hope in dance. I was glad to share this hope with my students. Dance strengthened my muscles, lessening my constant pain. It quieted my mind, giving me a sense of serenity. I was glad to share that, too.

It was as if dance was almost a cure for my mental and physical pain, a reassurance to my body that if I treated it with respect, that I would survive and be strong. Somehow, I already knew if kept my body strong, I could live with Sickle Cell Disease. Somehow, if we all could be strong, we could survive anything.

During this time, I stayed fairly healthy. Pain was overtaken by my newfound strength. Sickle Cell Disease, however, does increase the tendency for infections. Toward the end of that summer, after Kathy left, I got a really bad flu. As usual, I got no medical treatment, but I stayed in bed for two weeks and missed a few dance classes.

Kathy would never know how much she'd given me that summer. How she'd really saved my life when she introduced me to dance. That simple summer, I grew in confidence and strength. I learned to lead others by example and show others the hope I had also found. I also discovered I enjoyed teaching, mentoring young girls and expressing myself without fear.

I continued working for CETA for a few months becoming the baseball coach to my same group of dancing girls. With our new found teamwork, we successfully competed with other recreation centers, making it to the city-wide playoffs for their age group.

What a wonderful summer.

9
AGAINST THE ODDS

When school started that year, I was off to high school and my reputation as a gang member I had worked so hard to create preceded me. My fellow students already feared me. But dance had taught me that life was about more than fear.

I was tired of my hard exterior hiding a wounded core. I was ready to see good develop in my life. My friendship with the gang girls in my neighborhood ended as they saw me get closer and closer to dance. They didn't care to understand my attraction to it. It didn't fit their image of toughness so they left me alone.

When I worked at the Center teaching dance, I saved every dollar I made. I liked having money saved. After the baseball coaching job ended, I lined up another job as a salesgirl in a clothing store at the local mall, too. Each day, I walked 13 blocks to school, after school rode two buses' to work, worked until 10:30 p.m., and then rode two buses' home.

I loved getting clothes on discount and a paycheck too, but I didn't like the late nights on bus stops. One night, I was closing the store with my manager who was moving too slowly, and I missed my 10:35 p.m. bus home. I walked to the bus stop at 10:50 p.m. wondering how I was going to get home that night. My mother had no car, I knew no one who could pick me up, and so I just sat at the bus stop.

I watched a nearby restaurant's lights go out and its employees walk toward the bus stop too. A young man a little older than me walked up and said, "Hi." I smiled, "Which bus are you taking," I asked, hoping to find an alternate route home. "I'm taking the 210," he said, "It comes at 11:00 p.m." This was my bus number!

I thought I had missed the last bus at 10:35 p.m. Come to find out the *last* bus of the night was 11:00p.m. "Thank God," I thought. At 11:00 p.m. a bus pulled up and all us weary workers hopped on.

When I got to my second connector bus stop it was already 11:35 p.m. I knew I'd missed my earlier bus, so there was little chance I would have a ride home on my second bus. I sat on the bus stop bench anyway. I needed to gather my thoughts, figure out how long a walk I had ahead of me, and the best route.

Just then, a car full of laughing people stopped in front of me. The window rolled down and three laughing faces, one woman and two men, looked me over. A cloud of smoke floated out of the window as the woman said, "You need a ride?" I did need a ride but I looked into their faces and I hesitated. She noticed my eyes move from one man's face to the other. "Ah, they're not gonna hurt you," she said. "Get in!"

All of my senses tingled as she tried to ease my fear. I had enough street smarts to know they'd been drinking. I listened to my inner-self which prompted me not to move, and I didn't. Even though I didn't know how I was going to get home, I said, "No that's ok." The men looked at the woman, she squealed and the car speed away.

I got up from the bus stop bench and stood behind a bush near the stop. Praying to myself, "Lord help me get home safely." I then began to plot my long walk home. I put my purse under my coat and tightened the belt. Just before I took the first step, a bus turned the corner with my bus number on it. It was the midnight bus going my way.

I scurried back to the bus stop bench. As the doors opened, I looked up at the driver and smiled. He was an angel sent by God. I stepped up the stairs and he smiled back. "Is this the last bus?" I asked. "Yep, 12:00 a.m." he said. After flashing my pre-paid bus pass, I sat right behind the driver, finally feeling safe.

When I got home my mother and sisters were asleep. I got into bed without any one knowing or caring about my ordeal. That night, I believe I grew up in a whole new way. My instincts were tested, and I passed. I listened to my inner-self and it led me correctly. I shutter to think what would have happened to me if I'd taken that car ride. I just thanked God that I hadn't taken that ride from hell and that He provided me a safe way home.

Aside from my traveling trials, I felt hopeful again. My younger sister Kelly, left behind in junior high, was safe, now protected by my reputation. I could now let go of some of my worries about her safety. In high school, the high school gangs; knowing who my "big sister" was steered clear of me, and, I steered clear of any of their trouble too. I just wanted a new start leaving the gang stuff in my past.

My mother and older sister Macy were always fighting. Macy just couldn't forgive my mother for being poor, single, uneducated and uncaring. I, on the other hand, had accepted these facts and moved on. I stayed out of their fights about money and food, and made a way for myself. I liked working hard and getting paid for it, and I developed a relentless work ethic. With money in my pocket and a healthy body, I could feel at last my life was good.

Sometimes, however, my past would creep up and spoil my fun. At a party, someone who'd heard of my old street-kid past, would ask, "Were you in a gang?"

I would laugh it off as I moved through the crowd of partiers. I was ashamed of what I had been.

Still, I reminded myself it had all been about survival. A gang member had never been who I really was. I behaved like a gang member; it was not my true self. I behaved tough, although I was scared to death inside. I had been successful in the horrible classroom of life (Acting Like a Gang Member – 101) and passed with an A+. Now I just had to concentrate on moving on.

My high school was also a big contradiction to me. It was split in two, unofficially segregated—in this case, the Asians from blacks. We sat in class separately, ate lunch separately and even played separate sports: volleyball for Asians and basketball for blacks. While the Asian students studied gymnastics, black students took cheerleading. And while Asian students participated in academic clubs, most black students were noticeably absent.

Again, as I had been with the deaf children I went to school with when I was younger, I was to be in the middle. I was intrigued by the Asian students, fascinated at how they took time to study something and do it perfectly. I admired their work ethic and intellect. They'd never heard I'd been a gang member—and with them I could be my true self: funny, intelligent, thoughtful and kind.

My black friends, in contrast, knew of my past, encouraged me to skip class, get high, drink, and use school only for a place to hang out. I, however, had changed and had no interest in doing any of that.

I did have an interest in why races did not mix at my school. It was only when I began to observe the school staff that I noticed a trend. Asian students did better because they had a support system that black students didn't have. Their parents supported and encouraged them, school counselors guided their coursework towards college, and staff gave them privileges, like working in the library. The instructors took extra time to explain things to them without making them seem stupid for asking too many questions.

This was in contrast to what I noticed about black students. They were not encouraged at all. As I sat in the middle of this contradiction, I noticed the better I did in school, the more flack I got from my teachers.

Our biology instructor would write the names of students on the chalkboard that scored 100 percent on his exams. He would then allow them to pass out the next week's exam as a reward. Usually, only Asian students made 100 percent on his exams. When I scored 100 percent on an exam, the instructor added my name to the chalkboard, and my black classmates cheered. Then he smirked, walked pass me and handed the next week's exam to an Asian student near me.

After I scored 100 percent a few more times, he moved my desk to the front of the room, as if to prevent me from cheating. I worked hard in his class, taking personal pleasure out of making this instructor marvel at *my* ability to understand biology. I took his obvious displeasure with my success as a driving force to achieve.

In my school, black students were being left out and allowed to fail. It was assumed that classes like biology, chemistry, and calculus were just too difficult for us to learn. This made me mad. I too was a product of my environment. I had been raised impoverished, with no support system. I was supposed to fail. I knew, however, that I was capable of being a judge, a professor, even a doctor. But because the odds were against me, I was supposed to step back and let the leaders pass. I wanted to prove my teachers and counselors wrong. I vowed to show them that a black student who cared about her future could succeed.

And now that I recognized this new challenge in my life—this unfair, discriminatory treatment—I knew I could fight back. I could excel in my classes and join academic clubs without anyone's permission or support. I would explore dance through cheerleading and expose my soulful roots too. And I loved it. I was going to prove to teacher and the administrators that I would be more than what they allowed black students to be. I was going to expose the lie that being different means being inferior.

Initially, when I entered high school, my grades had slipped because of my working nights. But now, through late-night studying, I'd become a good student again. At first, most teachers couldn't believe how well I was doing, and reminded me of the school's cheating policy. I'd laugh, acing one test after another. Every time my name was added to a chalkboard, the instructor would look displeased, the Asian students curious, and the black students proud.

But not all of the teachers wanted me to fail. Impressed by my determination, some instructors told me about the conversations they'd had about me in the teacher's lounge. One teacher would argue I was pretending to be good but really a gang banging, bad girl. Then another would defend me, saying I was proof that anyone could change.

Their encouragement made me proud to be in this fight, the fight that only exists in the middle. I was no longer concerned that I "talked white," that I was "too black," or "not black enough." I was going to define myself, whether I was accepted or not. I'd found the middle ground between where the poor and disconnected compete with the well-supported and successful. Against the odds, I'd learned to push beyond what was expected of me.

I couldn't completely overcome my late start, my poor inner-city education left holes in some of my basic abilities like spelling and grammar. It left gaps in my knowledge of literature and history. I did, however, take classes my counselors discouraged like chemistry, psychology, and photography. I joined clubs where members dressed in matching green and pink suits. They outwardly wondered who invited me, yet offered to let me join. And, I got a kick out of joining the year book staff to make sure my memories of high school were also displayed.

In this inner-city high school I never did take a geography class. But when I look at a map, I always look for Luxembourg. I find that little country and remember that the capital of Luxembourg *is* in fact Luxembourg.

10
HOW IT FEELS

Two years had passed. I worked, went to school, danced semi-professionally and tried to stay healthy. It was a balancing act that I had grown accustomed to. To me, nothing was easy but I never complained. I had some sort of internal strength driving me to succeed. I was not going to be hungry, not going to be naked and never gonna fail if I could help it. I thought I had life all figured out.

Halfway through my senior year, having been offered scholarships to colleges all over the country, I decided instead to get married. I still can't explain the logic. Everything going my way meant, to my 17-year-old mind, that I had become an adult and could make adult decisions. I did have a problem looming over my head that could have encouraged my decision to get married.

My mother had a habit of giving her children their freedom when they turned 18-years old. This freedom really meant they had to get out of her house. I knew this was my fate too and I was afraid. Even though I had a possible way out, college, I took what I thought was a sure route. Marry a boy I didn't really know and make the biggest mistake of my young life.

My new husband was a boy I'd met through some friends and I'd only known him for six months. I thought I wanted to spend the rest of my life with him, but what did I know at 17?

Over the years, my recurring sickle cell 'crises' had given me a high tolerance for pain. But this decision to marry this man would cause me pain in a whole new way.

In December, before high school graduation, I told my mother I was getting married and needed her to sign a marriage license consent form. She did without any dispute. The ceremony was being planned by my future mother-in-law, to be held at her church. I didn't know anyone at the church, but they were excited to have a wedding, so all the church ladies pitched in to help. They offered to cater the food, buy the cake and flowers, and decorate the church.

My future mother-in-law suggested her sister make my wedding dress. I was told that her sister was a master seamstress and she would donate her talents as my wedding gift. I was excited and went to her house to be measured.

This woman's house was a landfill of objects. Everywhere I looked there were mounds of clothes, boxes, gadgets, and stuff. I was led to a room in the back of her house where a sewing machine and bolts of fabric was mound.

This woman seemed excited to be sewing my wedding dress, and giggled the entire time she measured me. I watched her face that looked very much like my future mother-in-law, noticing nothing out of the ordinary. She had high cheekbones and dark brown skin. I could tell she was a refined lady in her younger days, but seemed a little disorganized now. As I was measured, she turned me and stretched out my arms. I got a circular view of the mounds that surrounded me. I didn't think anything was odd about this women, considering odd was normal for me.

A few weeks passed after my initial measuring and I expected a call for a fitting. No call ever came. I asked my future mother-in-law about the fitting, but she assured me the dress would be done and fit perfectly. Being the good child-bride, I never brought it up again until the wedding day. The wedding was supposed to be at 1:00 p.m. At 11:00 a.m. I did not have a dress. At 11:30 a.m. my mother-in-law called and said I needed to go to her sister's house to *try-on* my dress.

I arrived around 12:00 p.m., in tears, and knocked on the door. This woman calmly opened the door and led me to her sewing room. She assured me that she would have the dress done in time for the wedding at 1:00 p.m. I started to remove my clothes to try-on my dress and she stopped me. "You don't need to take off your clothes," she said. "I just have to try these pieces on you." "PIECES!" I said.

To my horror, she placed cut out pieces of a dress up to my chest, along my legs, and around my arms. The dress was still in cut-out pattern pieces, not even sewn together.

I burst into tears. I could not believe what I was seeing. I was one hour away from my wedding and didn't even have a dress. I discovered what my mother-in-law already knew; this woman was having a mental breakdown AND she was sewing my wedding dress.

After the dress cutout try on, I left her house and drove right to the church. I sat in the ladies lounge in disbelief; I had no dress and the church was filling up with guest. An hour went by, then two, still no dress. I had no idea what to do. My future mother-in-law assured me that a dress would appear.

By this time, I thought everyone was crazy, and I no longer had any desire to get married. I began to ponder how to tell people the wedding was off. Just then, this woman runs into the ladies lounge with a dress covered in plastic. I couldn't even look at this woman. I didn't want to get married and didn't give a damn about that dress.

As the wedding march played, my future mother-in-law and the church ladies pushed me into the dress, then to the last isle entering the church. I looked down at my tan colored shoes that screamed "I don't match!" and my wedding dress that was too short. I looked like a child dressed up for a pretend wedding that never should have happened.

The wedding day passed me like a fog. I didn't hear anything or see anyone. I moved from one room to another; talking, eating and drinking, not really conscience of being there. A few of my sisters were there, in disbelief, and my mother sat off in the distance not involved in anything. This was my life as usual.

I finished high-school as the only married girl in my school. Of course, no one could believe what I'd done. My dance teacher was the only one who questioned my decision, which I defended adamantly. I started the marriage a self-assured, determined teenager with the whole world ahead of me, but that would not last long.

After graduation, instead of heading off to college, I enrolled in a local university. I assumed I would be able to work part-time and go to college as planned, but the reality of my marriage sank in. I questioned the logic of my decision.

Normally self-reliant, I began to resent feeling like a burden to a boy who really didn't understand what he'd done as well. I took one low-paying job after another, switching to night school. My resentment turned into dread. I began to dread my bad choice, and tried to leave returning only after he convinced me everything would change.

In high school, I'd danced on weekends in local dance troupes, but all that stopped. Without dance I started to get sick again as my body got weaker. It began with leg aches and then moved all over my body. I felt my life and joy slowly slip away.

Despite living in the middle of an unhappy marriage, my first child was my first ray of hope. It was without question I'd work during my entire pregnancy, and then go back to work immediately after the baby was born. I felt strong and sure that I could do it all, and by God I did.

During my daughter's birth a nurse told me, "PUSH" and then she bent my neck toward my knees. My legs went numb and I was paralyzed from the hips down. Childbirth is traumatic enough, but now I had a new baby and no feeling from the waist down. I was scared to death.

Doctor's came to my room with groups of medical students surrounding my bed. They poked my legs with pins that I didn't feel and discussed the complications of Sickle Cell Disease right in front of me.

After numerous tests', a neurologist determined that I had a sickle cell 'crisis' during child birth and a spinal nerve had been pinched. There was nothing we could do but wait. While my baby sat in the new born nursery, I started therapy.

First was message therapy, then heat treatments, and later physical therapy. My room was outfitted with arm slings to lift me up, and all I could think about was working hard to get my legs working again.

After the first few days I began to see progress. Each morning I'd get up, move my toes, rub my legs and try to bend my knees. Later in the week, I'd slowly pull myself with the sling, hang my legs over the side of the bed and dangle my feet. Finally, with help of a physical therapist, I pulled myself up from the bed and walked to the door.

The real test to see if I could go home was that I had to walk to the end of the hallway for a new mother's class. The hallway was no longer than normal, but it felt like the end would never come.

With the physical therapist behind me, I pulled myself up, walked slowly to the door, then out the door. I held on to the rail that was fastened to the wall all the way to the end. Nurses passed and smiled, "You're doing good," they said as they passed. I moved slowly, but determined to make it to the end of the hallway. Each step was a success, and one step closer to going home with my new baby.

After what seemed to be thirty minutes, I made it to the end of the hallway where the new mother's class was being held. When I got there, a group of nurses cheered me on from the nurse's station. I looked back to see a group of them watching my progress. I had made it.

The next day the doctor gave orders to send me home. "Go home," the doctor told me, "take care of your new baby."

Over the next few months I did just that. I was not going to let anything stop me from walking or taking care of my child. After a few months, I also went back to work.

Fearlessly, I became a tireless superwoman: taking my baby girl to the babysitter, then I'd go to work, then to school at night. In spite of my body's limitations, I decided I would not give up; I would carry the weight of this new life and succeed anyway.

Four years later, I gave birth to a son.

I fought upstream to manage my unbearable life. This included continuing to work, go to night school, and take care of now, two children. Quickly superwoman was about to get the shock of her life.

Though my body had remained strong from years of dance, I never got enough rest. I hadn't been drinking enough water and I rarely ate enough. My body was totally overextended.

One late night while studying, and burning the candle at both ends as usual, I felt a twitch of pain in my spine. I slid to the floor. The pain intensified into a sharp, stabbing pulses; like a murderer pressing a knife into my spine. Sickle Cell had come back with a vengeance. I was taken to the hospital and my children were taken to my mother-in-law's house.

When I arrived at the hospital, I first sat in a wheelchair in the emergency room lobby, twitching and moaning from the pain. Sickle cell 'crises' leave no outward sign of injury, but I cried out every time someone touched me. By the time I saw the on-call physician, he thought I was flipping out from some drug.

The doctor asked, "What is the problem tonight?" Although I could see and hear everything, the pain was so intense I could barely explain. As nurses poked and prodded me, trying to take my blood pressure, I finally managed to gasp, "I'M HAVING A SICKLE-CELL CRISIS!" Another physician bent over and looked in my eyes. "How do you know?" she asked. Despite my pain, I rose straight up from the bed and screamed, "I KNOW HOW IT FEELS!" After taking a blood sample, they left me in the examining room alone as I cried.

This experience showed me I knew nothing about pain. I had met the dragon of all sickle cell 'crises'. The pain was so deep in my spine I screamed out in agony. A nurse came by the room and simply closed the door.

When my cries became too disturbing, a nurse rolled my bed from the examination room to a dark room in the back of the emergency ward, and then closed that door. I was back in the closet again, trapped, with no one there to help me. I thought back to those nights when I cried out to my mother and my cries went unanswered. I remembered the feeling of dark pain, this night-time pain, where everybody was asleep except me. There, in the back of the emergency room, I rolled from side to side, trying to rock my pain to sleep.

After what felt like hours, a doctor I'd never seen came into the room. "Do you have Sickle Cell Disease?" she asked. Worn out from crying, I could barely speak. "Yes," I whispered. "Oh," she answered calmly. "You're having a sickle cell crisis."

Despite my pain, I had to laugh. Finally, I'd been heard. The doctor then ordered a nurse to turn the lights back on, give me oxygen, begin an IV of morphine for pain, and glucose for hydration. As the morphine began to work, I drifted off to sleep. It took two blood transfusions and a long week of recovery in the hospital before I felt better.

Before I was released from the hospital, that same doctor came to speak to me. I was sitting on my bed, dressed and ready to go, and she looked down at me and asked, "What did you do to yourself to get that bad?" I thought long and hard. I really didn't know.

I'd done what I'd always done. "I just go to work, school, and take care of my children," I told her. "What did you eat?" she asked. "Well, I often don't." I said, "But I drink lots of coffee." When I saw the look on the doctor's face, I immediately felt I should have known better. She looked at me seriously. "Do you want to die?" she asked.

Then, she began to tell me what I had to do if I wanted to live. I needed to drink water, not coffee, she explained, to keep my blood more fluid. I needed to rest more to let my body regenerate cells and restore energy. I needed to eat whole foods, not starve myself because I was too busy to eat. This doctor took the time to make sure I understood that if I didn't change the way I lived, I would die.

My childhood doctors had taught me what Sickle Cell Disease was, but they'd never told me how to live with it. Back then, my self-hatred was my greatest enemy, and those black doctors and nurses helped me accept my illness so that I could succeed despite it. I'd known my body was fragile, and thought by pushing myself, I was conquering the enemy in my body.

Now I saw that acting invincible was treating my body with abuse. I discovered I had to take part in caring for myself. My doctor's bedside visit helped me finally face the facts of my disease.

It was time for me to reject the notion that I was nothing unless I achieved something. I had two young children who relied on me, and I had to stay alive for them. I found that day, in that hospital room, I wanted to live for myself, too.

When I returned a week later for a doctor's follow-up visit, she commented on how well I looked. I replied, "The last time, you saw Sickle Cell Disease. Today, you're seeing me."

My mother and
father with my
eldest brother
(1941)

Me and my
grandparents
(1960)

Me in high school - cheerleader (1978)

Performing with dance troupe (1977)

Awarded Intern of the Year (1989)

Doing what I did best...WORK!

I kept this picture on my desk for 22 years.

My two children today

The love of my life-Rick

Three generations of strong women

What Sickle Cell Disease looks like in the blood

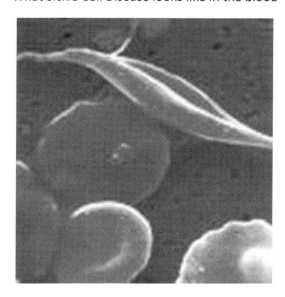

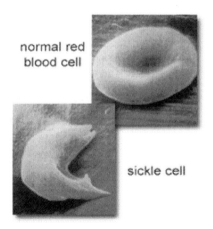

normal red blood cell

sickle cell

Education and Awareness

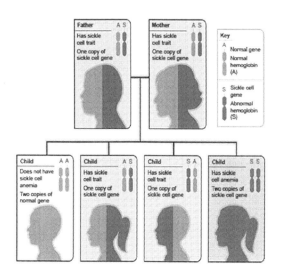

11
WATER BLESSING

My children were my only priority, and I wanted to live as their new, healthy parent. But my relationship with their father had only gone downhill. Without emotional or economic support, I was forced to go back to work after my hospital stay, but took time off from school to get rest.

It was getting expensive to live in Los Angeles. I wanted to give my children a better life and move out of the inner-city neighborhood. With school delayed, I focused on getting a better paying job.

While looking through the newspaper classified ads, something jumped out. An ad read, "Testing on Monday." Taking tests was no big deal to me, I was naturally good at it and I loved to challenge myself.

There was no job description, but I circled it and kept reading. When I looked over all of the ads I'd circled, this ad seemed interesting. I called and got all the testing information and planned to be the first person in line.

On the next Monday, I got up early, sent the kids to the babysitter, and rode the bus to the downtown Federal building. As planned, I was first in line. I was so adamant about giving my children a better life, getting up early and being the first in line was very important to me. I looked around the building and noticed a sign that read "United States Federal Human Resources Department."

When the office opened, they led everyone to a room full of desks, handed out test booklets, and gave us three hours to complete them. I still didn't know what the job entailed; my only concern was about the intended pay.

I began by completing the booklet questionnaire giving my name and contact information. When I began the test I noticed the questions involved basic math, reading comprehension, and office administration. The questions were so low-level I could tell they weren't specifically seeking someone with a high level of education, but I made sure to answer everything correctly anyway. I handed my test in and went off to two more interviews that day.

On Wednesday, they called—and offered me a job starting the following Monday. I still didn't know what the job was for or who I would be working for, but I knew I needed work. After asking about the starting pay amount, I accepted the job immediately.

I showed up for my first day of work at what turned out to be the Department of Defense Logistics Agency. This Agency is the buyer, manager, and distributor of all military defense products.

I was led to the Division Chief's Secretary who informed me that I would be *her* assistant. I looked at the organizational chart. My job title, Secretary Clerk, put me at the very bottom. For the next few months I researched ways to move up.

As I'd always done to make a place for myself in life, my first step was to observe the different groups. I noticed Managers always rushing to meetings and yelling at everybody. They seemed miserable. Young Interns called "Logistic Inspector Interns" involved in everything. They received the best training available. They seemed very interesting to me.

The veteran Inspectors were rarely in the office—most of their work took place in the field. When they did come into the office, they joked around and seemed happy. I concluded this inspector job deserved further investigation.

I started by simply asking as few Inspectors, "How did you get this job?" I took note of their answers. Most had completed degrees, which I did not have. But some had entered through the Inspector Intern Program.

This program was funded to open the ranks of the workforce to women and minorities. I heard one "educated" black co-worker call the Intern program a "welfare" program. That didn't bother me. I needed a ticket in. *That* was my ticket in.

Most of the Inspector Interns were women and minorities. This was in the 1980s, when minorities were very scarce in high-level corporate jobs, and women were considered even less appropriate in executive positions.

Certainly, I was in the middle of both of these seats. Most times, my co-workers didn't know I was black because of my fair skin color. But, I made sure they knew. I wanted to be a good example for both my race and my gender. I figured, if I was going to fight stereotypes, why not fight them all. Luckily, times were changing and performance was the measure being used.

I saw this Inspector Intern program as a career as opposed to just another job. After six months as a Secretary Clerk, I applied for the internship program, with the promise to finish my degree, and was hired. I found out that I needed to be versed in higher level math, science, engineering, and software science. Most of my prior education had been geared toward business, so I went back to night school.

Thus began my three year journey of night classes in electrical engineering, mechanical and software science, and operations management. At the end, I graduated from Secretary to Inspector—but unlike most of my young, just-starting-out colleagues, I had a life-threatening illness and two children in tow.

I kept my little secret about having Sickle Cell Disease to myself. No one had to know, I concluded. It took effort to prevent illness and I never let it show when I did feel pain. I wanted to prove that I could accomplish something if given the chance. I worked hard trying to prove I belonged.

I felt constant pressure to not fail. My co-workers didn't understand the source of my ambition, but my two babies did. They needed diapers, milk, food, clothes and love. I was determined to provide what they needed.

My new job was far more exciting than my work as a Secretary. As an Inspector, I was responsible for auditing quality assurance policies and procedures at a number of defense contractor companies throughout Southern California.

After three years in training as an Intern, my first real Inspector assignment turned out to be with a major aircraft manufacturing company that built cargo planes for the federal government. My job was to inspect their development processes of automatic flight-control software and testing practices.

It was my first assignment, and I was committed to proving that *I* could turn the company around. In two years of auditing this company, I didn't make a dent. The company's poor management had crippled their quality assurance practices. When I found out that a test plane had almost crashed in the desert during a flight—with two different flight control computers and two different software versions were on the same plane—I don't know how I didn't go crazy.

The company kept denying wrongdoing and the government was furious. My office (me) was again sent in to "clean things up."

This time around I became more aggressive. I read every procedure, and then traced their employees' steps to make sure they followed them. I watched every software test, looking for any hint of error. I tracked every flight control computer's movement throughout the company, ensuring accountability and traceability.

Finally, the company knew they had to work with me, not against me. I was able to persuade them to improve their methods of operations based on recommendations for better control and safety. We saw an immediate turnaround.

My manager called me into her office, I assumed to commend me for my hard work. Instead, she smiled and said, "Great news! The pilots requested that you fly with them on Thursday's test flight."

When I heard the request, fear washed over me. It's not that I wasn't confident in having improved the company's safety procedures. I knew I had done a good job. These flights were called "test" for a reason—the planes weren't fully built. Anything could go wrong! And all I could think about was that near crash—and my children.

My manager listened, as I explained why I wasn't the right person to go on this important test flight. She then brushed off all of my reasons. It was settled. Thursday, I would fly.

On Wednesday, during my usual pre-flight inspection, I uncovered mistakes and oversights of all kinds, and I was supposed to fly on that very plane. I worked all day to get those issues resolved.

On test flight day, I usually had no trouble getting to work at 4 a.m. On this Thursday morning, the day of *my* dreaded flight, everything moved slower. I didn't care if I was late. In fact, I hoped I would be.

On this morning, fog hovered over the highway, and street lights reflected water crystals in the air. The morning felt eerie, like the opening scene of a horror movie. Unconsciously, I drove not aware of on-ramps or off-ramps. I drove, then blinked, and found myself driving toward the office near the runway for the early morning pre-flight meeting.

When I arrived at the pre-flight meeting, the room was already full. All eyes turned toward me as I walked in. I was wearing tight jeans and a white t-shirt; they were wearing a military issue green jumpsuit. I stood out like a red dress in a sea of black. Not only had I not yet been given my green jumpsuit, I was also the only woman in the room.

As I walked to my seat, I caught a glimpse of myself in a mirror—my hair in pony tail, no make-up, not even lip gloss. I saw a glimpse of a girl from the ghetto reflected in that mirror—and I had to laugh about how far I'd come.

As the speaker discussed test flight operations and showed graphs and charts, my thoughts drifted to my mother. Would she be proud of me, I wondered? Looking around the room I thought, "Would she see this moment in my life as insignificant?"

My mind drifted as I thought about my life. How I survived our bad neighborhood. How I excelled in school in spite of no encouragement or support. How I was overcoming my illness.

I was about to take part in an amazing test flight, in a cutting-edge military aircraft, doing something few Americans would ever experience, especially a black women raised in poverty like me. I wondered if my mother would even care.

Suddenly, the meeting was over and someone handed me a military green jumpsuit to put on. The pilot, looking like a less-handsome version of Tom Cruise in *Top Gun*, introduced himself. He looked at bit cocky, but not obnoxious. His eyes, brown and green under bushy eyebrows, shined with confidence. His face was young, chubby, and clean-shaven. He shook my hand with a strong grip, but warmly, and when I smiled, his chest rose a bit, like a good soldier. His presence was gentle yet commanding, and my fears dissolved.

My walk on the tarmac was cold and fog-covered. Through the fog I could see a series of high-voltage lights, lighting the way to a gray colored plane in the mist, only visible because of the red lights flickering on its large body. It sat like a beached whale, its wings like massive fins, the open cargo ramp like a mouth hanging open. Each step I took towards it, I wanted to run back two.

As I entered the cockpit, the pilot motioned for me to sit behind the co-pilot. I pulled the folded seat down and sat. I put my helmet on and checked the sound to make sure I could hear conversations going on. Now, I was seeing life from the pilot's perspective.

Looking through one of the large four windows, I could look down and see people packing up their trucks and rolling off the tarmac. I looked up, and two smaller windows on the roof were patches of sky, now blue. Dozens of gauges, dials, levers and buttons blinking red and green were within my reach. I thought, "I'm really here."

When the pilot pushed a lever forward and the engine roared, I gasped. The smell of jet fuel flooded the cockpit, and vents pushed clean air to replace it. The tower crackled, "You're good to go," and we taxied down the runway at high speed. When the pilot pulled a large lever near his right hand as we lifted off the ground, I held my breath again. That beached whale had floated effortlessly into a horizontal climb.

The plane banked to the left, over the airport, toward the ocean, which was bluer than the sky. I looked toward the coastline and saw rolls of white water crashing onto the shores. I saw blocks of squares that outlined streets, then smaller squares that defined houses and businesses. Familiar things looked entirely different, and everything sparkled like a Christmas toy.

Military aircraft can fly lower than commercial aircraft, and we came down close to Catalina Island. Horses raced beneath us, while trees seemed to reach up to touch our wings. The sun felt warm on my face. I pinched myself. How had my life taken me *here*?

Two hours later, after completing our flight tests, we headed back. This large military aircraft would one day see combat in a war zone or deliver food to hungry people in Africa. I was proud to be part of her maiden voyage.

In keeping with military tradition, as I exited the cockpit and stepped onto the tarmac, the pilot and flight crew dumped a bucket of water over my head to christen me after my first flight.

I couldn't stop thinking of the moment over Catalina Island, when the pilot looked over his shoulder and, seeing my childlike delight, smiled. All the pieces of my life, I realized, had led me to *this* moment. I didn't need anyone to validate me anymore. I belonged.

When I got back to my office no one had to ask how the flight went. They could see by the smile on my face that I had been to heaven and seen angels. My manager simply nodded, "I knew you would enjoy it," she said. I was so happy that I had faced my fears and overcome them.

12
GRAND ADVENTURE

After finally deciding I would be better off single, I entered a bitter custody battle for my children. A judge managed to separate my two children. My son was ordered to live with his father, my daughter with me. This struggle was damaging to all of us. I wanted to protect my children in this adult matter, so I remained silent about the details of what I'd lived through with their father.

Despite fighting over child custody and the like, my career was moving ahead. I was finally focused on providing my children a better life and moving over the past. While starting my life over, I met a wonderful man. Although, he was gentle and kind, I was afraid to trust anybody. It took him a lot of work for him to break through my armor of protection. When he did, we were inseparable.

About this time, my father died. I had managed to drive to the hospital in San Diego, California, before he passed. When I stood over his bed, I felt I was looking at a stranger.

I held out my hand. He grabbed it. "Edna," he said. My brother Harold corrected him; "This is not Edna." My father looked weary from pain. "She looks like her mother," he finally said. Silently holding his hand, I wondered if he ever thought about my sister Cynthia, his daughter, who died needing a blood transfusion. I never had the chance to ask him if he regretted preventing that blood transfusion. Being that it was too late now, we stood quietly in the dark, and I said goodbye to a stranger. Days later he died.

While my father was still at the morgue, I discovered that he had no money for a funeral. My brother Harold, whom I also barely knew, informed me that cremation was not an option. I called around to each of my father's children. One by one, they had an excuse for not wanting any part of burying him. I was disappointed at their shallow excuses.

All my life, my father never really did anything for me. He had no idea what I'd been through in my childhood, how my mother blamed *us* for *his* actions. He didn't rescue me from poverty or care when I was in kid's jail. But I believed, like any other human being, he deserved a proper burial.

I called a mortuary that my mother-in-law used to arrange her husband's funeral. When I made the appointment, I had no idea what I was doing. I drove there after work and definitely didn't want to be there after dark. The office was deep in the south-side of Los Angeles where darkness brought out the worse people.

The mortuary was small and clean. As I walked into the lobby, I could see actual body's laying-in-wait in separate rooms. The receptionist greeted me with a warm smile, and then led me to a small office. "I'm sorry for your loss," she said. "Thank You," I replied, not knowing how to show emotion for the loss of someone I didn't know.

Large books with pictures of caskets were set in front of me on the desk. I turned pages quickly, noticing price lists at the end. Then, books of flower arrangements were spread in front of me. I thumbed through those just as fast. All the while, I wondered how I was going to pay for anything.

The funeral director came into the office and noticed my uncertainty. He began to gently direct me toward making choices. I chose a casket, the best I could afford, and flowers. I signed papers to authorize transportation of my father's remains from San Diego to Los Angeles.

I could not believe I was making these choices for my father, especially since my step-mother was still alive and able to make these choices for him. Everyone in my family stepped aside and waited for me to get it all done.

After signing the papers, I remembered my brother Harold notified me of a request *he said* my father wanted. "Dad wants to be buried next to Cynthia," he said plainly. Without missing a beat, I informed the funeral director of this special request. He promptly notified me, "We don't handle burial. We help plan the funeral and prepare the body." Burial involved something else entirely.

I was told to find out where my sister Cynthia was buried, and then see if the cemetery had a space for my father. Of course, this meant more money I didn't have. I left the office emotionally numb and physically drained.

The next day I called Harold to ask where Cynthia was buried. He told me where, and I called the cemetery to explain my situation. The cemetery surprisingly was close to my new work office in Burbank, so I drove there after work. This office was formal with gold leaf pictures and old drapery hanging from the windows. It felt old and morbid.

The attendant who met with me looked 20 pounds too thin, and had an odd expression on his face the entire time. He led me to a gold trimmed office, and again, books came out. Books full of headstone pictures. The attendant took my sister's name and left me alone while he searched burial plot records. I looked at the headstone prices, and then closed the book. In minutes he came back and said, "I found your sister and we *do* have room for your dad." I exhaled in relief.

The attendant sat down and pulled out a price sheet. I watched his mouth move, but didn't hear any words. I had to come up with more money to buy the burial plot space. I blinked and came back to reality when he said, "Let's go out to see the plot."

We drove on a golf cart through manicured lawns. We stopped at the farthest corner in the back of the cemetery. We found my sister Cynthia's unmarked grave only because it had numbers listed on a dial mounted on top. I looked at the grave, its location and felt disgusted. The attendant could see my distain and promptly said, "This area was for people who couldn't pay for a funeral. The County of Los Angeles paid for these plots for the poor." I looked down at the dry brittle grass, and for the first time, I felt her loss.

We returned to the office, agreed to a price, and signed papers to have my dad buried, as he wished, in the grave next to Cynthia.

The funeral was uneventful. No tears were shed and only four of his children came. His wife and my step-sister came as well, but they shed no tears either. I watched the funeral as if from a distance, separate from it. Wishing I could have done more. I wished I could have afforded more flowers, a better casket, or tears.

I drove to the cemetery, not wanting any part of the one limo I paid for. A few words were said and everyone left. I remained a moment, took a flower from my father's casket, and placed it on my sister's grave. I said a prayer, blessing her memory, knowing now I understood her pain.

After that ordeal, I needed to get away. I signed up at work for an on-the-job training class that would take me anywhere. I was really signing up for a free trip away from my life.

Shortly after, I received notice at work I'd be taking a two-week class in Phoenix, Arizona. Leaving the kids with my mother-in-law, I got out of town.

Arizona has a reputation for dry heat, but Phoenix summers are muggy, filled with monsoons crackling with lightning and thunder. The first week it rained then switched back to 99-degree hot soup. Finally, that first weekend, the weather cleared up, moist ground revealing budding cactus flowers everywhere.

I had a classmate I'll call Firecracker, old enough to be a grandmother, but up for anything. She was from Oregon and had never seen the Grand Canyon, so we agreed to a road trip, and set off on Saturday morning for our adventure.

Our trip began in Phoenix and wound up highway 17 through Scottsdale, where track houses, surrounded by gravel landscaping, sat baking in the sun. The highway was deserted. Hitting the desert, we saw Arizona's state plant; Saguaro Cactus dotted everywhere, reaching up toward heaven with buds of red-flesh colored fruit. The drive became increasingly breathtaking. We passed hills covered with Teddy Bear Cholla, the cactus bush that changes color in the sunlight. Then, a sea of sticky, prickly cactus stalks, where nature at its most primitive, fanned out despite the heat.

We had already made reservations to stay at a small hotel in a town past Flagstaff at the bottom of the canyon. We planned to have dinner there and then spend the night. After arriving and eating dinner, my head started to pound. I bought a large bottle of water at the gift shop, took three aspirin, and threw up my dinner. I could do nothing but crawl into bed.

In the morning, I woke up excited to see the Grand Canyon. My head pounded. I drank two extra cups of coffee with three more aspirins, and Firecracker and I got on the road. Here, the ride to the Grand Canyon was less scenic, and straight up. The car felt like it was at a 90-degree angle. With each turn of the wheel, I felt myself get weaker and weaker.

By the time we saw the sign "Grand Canyon," I hardly cared. While Firecracker jumped into high gear, I moved completely into slow motion. I felt my body breaking down.

I didn't want Firecracker to worry, so I forced a smile. The first Canyon lookout had no railing, but Firecracker jumped straight onto a boulder so I could take her picture. I could barely drag myself out of the car.

Still, looking through the camera lens, I saw something miraculous: the earth's core. The colorful soil changes marked rows of earth's history. I looked out as far as my eye could see and I saw God's work. I took every detail of this magnificent sight in. I wanted to burn this memory in forever. By then, Firecracker had jumped off the boulder. "Let's drive along the rim and see some more!" she cried.

For the rest of the day, I didn't get out of the car. My body was so weak I could barely whimper, "No," when Firecracker asked if I was okay.

We both had to be in class the next morning, and we had the long drive in front of us. Firecracker put the car on auto-pilot at 90 miles an hour. Needless to say, when a Trooper's siren came, I was fully expecting it. When the officer asked for her license and registration, she said, "I'm sorry," then smiled. "My friend is sick, and I need to get her back to Phoenix." The officer was not impressed. With ticket in hand, we drove the rest of the way in silence.

When we got back, I practically rolled out of the car, returning to my air-conditioned hotel only to sleep past eleven the next morning. I didn't even care that I was missing class. I was taking aspirin, drinking water, and throwing up. I thought about going to the hospital, but I was alone in a strange city, so I roughed it out.

After two days of sleep and a meal that finally stayed down, I felt well enough to go to class. My instructor took one look at me and became sympathetic. "No one has to know you missed two days of class," he said. I was so thankful because I would have to repeat the class all over again.

After finishing out the week, I returned home. I still had no idea why I had gotten sick. The sickness I endured felt like food poisoning with vomiting, fever, chills, and headache. I didn't realize the Grand Canyon was at an elevation of over 8,000 feet. High elevation reduces the amount of oxygen available to breath. Less oxygen causes people with sickle cell disease to suffer with multiple illnesses, possibly leading to death.

I now know I could have gone into a full-blown sickle cell 'crisis' because of the high elevation. I had been lucky once again. I fought the illness to get back to class, but looking back I could have died alone in my hotel room. God knows, I should have never seen the Grand Canyon with my own eyes. I guess ignorance was bliss.

13
RESTING POSE

The stress of being shuffled back and forth between homes was difficult for my children. Both were placed in a position to have to "choose," and it caused us sickness and separation.

Eventually, our life settled down, but without my son. While the fight between my children's father and I raged for years, I married that wonderful man (Rick) who watched the entire mess.

This kind, tolerant man became the love of my life and my soul mate. He loved all of my flaws, my sickling blood, my aches and pains, and soothed them all. He forced me to rest when I tried to do everything on my to-do list, and made me smile when pain reared its ugly head. He rubbed my back, my legs, my arms, and my heart.

During this time, I was so blessed to have Rick in my life. I believe I remained strong and survived it all because of the love he shared with me. Thankfully, we kept our love as the foundation of our relationship, as we joined forces to protect my children and our marriage.

Eventually, my children and I made peace with our lives. We learned to cling to each other for support. I prayed for my son to learn *good* things about me by watching my actions. And, I had to forgive their father for everything he did or did not do.

In the mists of this messy personal life, I continued to pursue my career with diligence. I moved up the ladder quickly to better-paying jobs. I always loved science and dreamed of one day working with the National Aeronautical Space Agency (NASA).

While surfing the internet I stumbled upon a government job announcement for NASA. The job fit me like a glove. Over the years I had changed career paths from Aviation Inspector to Contract Procurement, so my background was full of diverse experience in electronics, software design and procurement for the Government.

I daydreamed about working with NASA. While inspecting mechanical and electronic systems on the Space Shuttle Endeavor, I dreamed of traveling to space to inspect the International Space Station. But, considering I couldn't even go to the Grand Canyon, that was an impossible dream.

This job with NASA was the next best thing.

I put everything I had in to this application. I held back nothing. I wrote like I ruled the world, describing all the wonderful experiences I had gained in 15 years while working for the Defense Department. I was confident what God had for me, I was going to get. Nothing, I thought, was too big for me. I sent all 75 pages of the application to the address in Washington D.C. Two weeks later I was called for an interview.

Besides the fact I got lost and was late, which are both unlike me; I was ready for this interview. I had my Oleg Cassini suit on, and my list of questions to ask *them*.

When I walked into the interview, 15 minutes late, I apologized, and sat down. Even though I was horrified that I had just committed a sure "no hire" error of being late, I had to stay composed. My application was on the desk in front of the woman interviewing me. She asked questions that I knew were on my resume, but I answered them like she was an old friend and we were having a casual conversation.

After the interview she walked me over to meet the Director, who was an ex-astronaut, and everyone else on the team. I was told they would notify me when they made their decision. I was happy with my performance and knew I gave my best. The rest was in God's hands.

Two months went by, nothing. Three months passed and I didn't even get a "no thank you." I was crushed. During this time I really prayed. God always heard my prayers and I relied on him for everything in my life. I prayed over my children, my marriage, my home, everything. But this time there was silence.

At the beginning of the fourth month, I couldn't take the silence any more. I called the woman who interviewed me. "I interviewed with you four months ago," I said. "I was wondering if you notified all the applicants yet?" The phone went silent. "You never got a call?" she asked. "No," I said, feeling bad news coming soon. "Someone should have called you; you start on the 23rd of January."

I was hired. Not only to my dream job, but as the first black executive in this NASA Procurement office.

My life was becoming everything I envisioned it could be, a success. Overall, life was hard, but looking brighter everyday. I worked on the most exciting space related procurement issues and managed major programs related to software systems. Fighting stereotypes all along the way, I was fulfilled that my hard work did pay off in the end.

My children were doing fine. They had graduated from high school, and then went on to college. I started looking forward to retirement and finally, rest.

I moved out of Los Angeles to a small town near the Sequoia National Forest. I continued to work for NASA, by telecommuting, only driving to the office once a week for meetings. The rest of the week, I worked from home and concentrated on staying healthy. I thought I was finally on track.

Slowly, feeling guilty for being away from the office, my workaholic side began to cause me to overcompensate. I was responsible for millions of dollars worth of NASA financial software system data. Being that I was the only black person working in this NASA office, my performance was always under a microscope. I cared about performing this job with my normal pursuit of perfection, even if it killed me. While working at home I barely took a break. I ate, drank and worked right there at my desk for ten hours a day.

At the same time, my job also required that I travel to Washington D.C. once a month. This is when I started having problems with my legs. My joints would lock in different positions, and my bones would crack. I would always have some pain somewhere in my body, but I was used to that.

I thought I needed more exercise. I joined a gym and starting taking yoga classes for relaxation. Little did I know lack of circulation in my legs was making my blood flow decrease. Exercise would help the matter, but Sickle Cell Disease had other silent destruction going on.

During one trip, as I made a run for a flight, I felt my right hip actually crack. I stood at the gate of my now-missed flight, tears running down my face. The woman standing behind the ticket counter looked concerned. "I'm sorry you missed your flight," she said. She had no idea I was in terrible pain.

It was the beginning of a week's worth of travel I had left on my itinerary, with meetings scheduled every day. As the airline clerk re-scheduled me on the next flight, I gulped down three jumbo aspirin, still weeping. I limped through the next week, nearly overdosing on painkillers and prayer.

Upon my return, I went to the doctor and was diagnosed with a degenerative bone disease in both hips, Avascular Necrosis. This is a complication of Sickle Cell Disease where the joints of the body decay due to lack of oxygen to the bone. As the weeks passed, these small cracks would occur more and more frequently. It was as if my disease wanted me to remember its presence. "Don't forget about me!" it was saying. "I'm still here!"

Though I was working at home by telecommuting, something had to be done. I hadn't yet reached the age of retirement, and my job was very important to me. I couldn't let those cracking bones slow me down, so pain killers became my way to keep going.

I fell into a rhythm; work, travel, rest. I thought I had the pattern at the right setting to stay healthy.

I assured Rick I was able to keep up the pace and would rest more than I liked. My workaholic side, however, kept creeping up. One year after my airport adventure, ironically, my body broke down in a yoga class.

I was sitting in a yoga resting pose with the lights out and soft sounds of water flowing. My body so relaxed that it felt like I was melting into the mat. But when my instructor said class was over, I found I couldn't move and couldn't speak. A twitch moved up my right foot, into my right knee, and then shot up to my right hip. This pain didn't grow slowly. It screamed, "I'M HERE!"

Luckily, I told the instructor weeks earlier that I had degenerative bone disease, specifically in my hips. As she walked around the room, noticing I hadn't moved, she took her warm hands, placed them on my lower back, and pressed them up toward my shoulders.

As she rubbed, the pain seemed to slide off my body. The other classmates had already rolled up their mats and left the room. The instructor rubbed and pushed, pushed and rubbed. After a few minutes I was able to stand. Little did she know that her touch had saved my life. A break from the pain gave me the opportunity to go home and get real help.

I drove home immediately to grab my medical records, and tell Rick to take me to the hospital. Because he'd never seen me in a full sickle cell 'crisis',

I tried not to scare him. But he saw the look on my face and fear flooded his. Already, I couldn't put any weight on my right leg, so he had to carry me to the car.

His calm broke down immediately. We hit a tree stump in our yard, and then drove over the speed limit toward the hospital. I couldn't concentrate because of his erratic driving. The pain had started stabbing me with its full fury. I closed my eyes and went inside myself, as I'd done many times before to cope with pain.

When we reached the hospital, a line awaited us stretching out the front door. While I sat in the car rocking my pain, Rick, as he told me later, walked past the line, went inside, and asked for a wheelchair.

The nurse behind the counter ignored him and continued to chat with another nurse. He waited for a moment, then asked again politely, "May I get a wheelchair for my wife in the car?" The nurse looked at him and said, "Wait your turn!" And then, as he told me, he snapped. He yelled. He cursed. He screamed, "I WANT A WHEELCHAIR NOW!" Another nurse quickly grabbed one and said, "Where is your car?"

I couldn't stand for anyone to touch me, so I lifted myself out of the car. Rick handed my medical record binder to the doctor and simply said, "Sickle cell, right knee and hips!" The doctor nodded and walked out of the room, thumbing through the binder. As I rocked back and forth in pain, he came back quickly with instructions for the nurse to start oxygen, and morphine and glucose drips. He then ordered X-rays and MRIs of my right knee and hips. We discovered the cartrilge in my right knee and both hips was fully decayed.

Sickle Cell Disease was now laying claim to my bones. I was admitted into the hospital for the usual routine of pain treatment and hydration, and then sent home after a week to rest.

My only treatment option was having one or both hips replaced. Eventually, I was informed, the knee would also need this treatment. Pain was now going to be constant and my mobility was going to change dramatically. I opted to postpone the surgery, finding herbal and alternate treatments for the pain and mobility issues.

Ironically, it was in my yoga class, where I went to relax, that my body took a nose dive. Even my supposed healthy exercise would expose the limitations of my body. I decided to retire from my demanding job at NASA, finally excepting the truth about Sickle Cell Disease and its ever increasing complications.

14
KEEP LAUGHING

Despite the difficulty Sickle Cell Disease has caused me, I try to laugh about it whenever I can. There are times when my patience is tested, but I also try to keep a good attitude. This good attitude, however, was put to the test at my son's college graduation.

My son, attended college in Utah. At 4400 feet, Utah is at a much higher elevation than Los Angeles, and I was concerned about visiting him. Before making a trip to see him, I spoke to my doctors and they suggested I drive to Utah first to allow my body to gradually get acclimated to the elevation changes.

Early one autumn day, before my son started his sophomore year, my husband, son and I drove the beautiful 12 hour drive to Utah. We drove through the Tehachapi Pass with its tan colored mountains. I was excited to see my son's temporary home. Driving past Barstow, California towards Las Vegas, the desert was calm after an unquestionably hot summer. We stopped in Las Vegas for gas, water, and a quick pull on a dirty slot machine with no luck.

As we left Las Vegas driving toward the Nevada border, I watched elevation road signs noting the numbers were rising. I took over the job as driver to distract myself from worrying about elevation changes. Rick slept in the back seat, getting a well deserved rest. My son knew of my concern, so he distracted me with small talk the rest of the trip.

As we entered the state of Utah, the drive was smooth, the landscape was breathtaking. With red mountain tops and golden soil, the landscape resembled that of the planet Mars. With barren rock formations formed in pre-historic times, the only thing I could compare it to was the beautiful Grand Canyon.

Despite watching every elevation sign, where some rose to the maximum of 6,200 feet, I kept driving and my son kept talking. Exactly 12 hours later, we arrived.

After my first visit, I discovered I could tolerate the elevation in Utah, for a short period of time, without any sickle cell related illness. After that first trip without illness, I flew to Utah to visit him a few more times. Each time I would visit it was late summer or early autumn.

In December of his senior year, my son was scheduled to graduate with the winter class 2007. Having gone to summer school each year, he had accumulated many more units than required. So, in his senior year, he only needed two classes to graduate. I was so excited that he'd finished college, and of course, I planned to attend his graduation.

I knew Utah had harsh winters, and being in December, there was no guarantee that weather would be good enough for travel. Even though I knew there might be more than a foot of snow on the ground, I was going to see my baby walk across that stage. Rick and I made plans for the weekend trip and was set to meet my daughter at Salt Lake City International airport.

When I checked the weather the day before our flight from Los Angeles, sure enough, it was 30 degrees with snow on the ground. I wasn't worried about Rick, who was born on the East Coast and knew how to deal with severe winter conditions.

I packed sweaters, winter coats, gloves, hats, and anything else I could think of to make sure I'd stay warm. We boarded the plane at L.A International Airport, in seventy-degree weather, wearing coats and hats. Sure enough, as we flew over the snow-capped Rocky Mountains, white snow stretched as far as I could see. I was filled with joy over the magnificent beauty I was witnessing.

I was also so thankful that my son and I had overcome the tragedy of our broken home. While he was in college, we had gotten the opportunity to get to know each other away from the child custody battles. As an adult, he was free to be himself and be a part of my life again. I was thankful God had let me live to see that moment.

We landed in Salt Lake City, where it was a sunny, hot eighty-degrees, with snow on the ground. (Go figure.) By the time we got our luggage, a rental car and we're on the highway, the weather started to change to something closer to what I'd seen reported. As we drove from Salt Lake City to a small town one hour north, night approached and the temperature began to drop further. Snow began to fall hard.

Rick, experienced with driving in snow, was calm and enjoying the drive. I, on the other hand, was anxious as flakes of snow turned into clumps. The mountains, valleys and roads were becoming completely covered with white powder. The hour-long drive to the hotel turned into a three-hour ordeal. My daughter sat in the back seat, texting her friends from her cell phone, oblivious to my panic. Three hours later, we checked into a Holiday Inn, exhausted from the days travel.

The next morning, we woke to news reports of 23-degree weather and deep snow drifts from the all-night storm. Since the school was only blocks away, I didn't worry about the weather. I was unbelievably happy. As I got dressed I started to get a mild headache. Two aspirin later, I was fine. Then, as we drove to the college my mind became scattered. I couldn't read the directions and began to feel a little sick.

Regardless of feeling a little odd, I pressed on. During the ceremony, I cried the entire time. Though I was feeling dizzy and nauseous, I cried tears of pride, and pain. By the time they called my son's name, my head was pounding. Because this was my son's special day, I pushed on, swallowing three more aspirin and continuing to snap pictures.

Afterwards, we attended a dinner hosted by the Alumni Association, and then went to the movies. Through it all I felt dizzy. My daughter noticed how unbalanced I walked and instinctually grabbed my arm to help me keep my balance. Suddenly, I was grouchy, my headache returning despite the aspirin I'd swallowed. I forced myself to stay together to share the day with my children, but now I was going downhill quick. I couldn't deny that something was wrong.

After the day's events, I went back to the hotel to rest while everyone else attended a basketball game that night. I prayed for God to get me back home. I knew I had to get out of Utah and convinced myself to be strong. I needed to get back home to my doctors, quick. The next day we were leaving and all I had to do is make it through the night.

The next morning I felt a little better. We said goodbye to my son, who was staying behind to settle his affairs. A big storm was expected later that night, but we drove to the airport in good weather. My daughter had made separate travel plans, so we waved goodbye to her as she took off to her non-stop flight to Los Angeles. Me and Rick's flight included a layover in Atlanta.

Our first flight from Salt Lake City to Atlanta took off on-time. In Atlanta, we waited nearly two hours for our plane to arrive, delayed by an East Coast snow storm. While in departure, I'd started to get the chills, and was finding it difficult to breathe. Because of the weather extremes, hot in LA, cold in Utah, I thought, I was simply getting a cold, and put on my coat and started drinking hot tea. The plane, when it finally arrived, was warm and cozy, and I bundled up more and immediately fell asleep.

When I woke up in flight, I couldn't breathe at all. I was covered with sweat. I reached up to open the vent above my seat, but they were all turned off. I snatched my heavy coat off, and threw my hat, scarf and gloves off too. I stood up from my seat, gasping, and made my way desperately down the aisle, people looking at me, startled, as I roughly pushed past their stretched-out legs.

In the bathroom, I splashed as much water as I could on my face, then lifted my shirt to wet my stomach and shoulders. I opened the bathroom door and

125

waved the flight attendant over, asking him to please get me ice water AND turn on the air. He paused and sighed, as if he already had enough to do. I went back to my seat to wait. He brought me no water, and the air stubbornly refused to come on. Rick, just waking up from his mid-flight nap, "Are you okay?" he asked. At thirty-thousand feet in the air, panicking, I said, "NO!"

What I didn't know was that the air in Utah is thinner during winter. I'd been visiting my son in summer and autumn, and because my body had received enough oxygen during those months, I was fine. But for this entire weekend, my body had been lacking a critical amount of oxygen.

All my symptoms—headache, dizziness, irritability, hot and cold chills—were identical to those which cause elevation sickness. The thin winter air of Utah created the same problem, and was as damaging to my system as being at a higher elevation.

By the time we landed in Los Angeles, my condition had reached a breaking point. I was taken immediately to the hospital, where I was quickly given oxygen and two blood transfusions. This trip, and over exposure to high elevation, caused irreversible sickle cell related damage to my body.

My spleen was three times larger than any doctor attending me had ever seen. I noticed their shock as they touched my now protruding stomach. I, too, felt the swollen spleen float in my abdomen like a baby floating out of place. Every touch caused pain.

Rick told me later, I was really bad off. When nurses asked me questions, I answered like I was drunk, slurring my words. My bottom lip drooped to one side, not moving as it should have. When nurses took me to the bathroom, my left leg dragged behind me. I had suffered a minor stroke.

A week later, still in the hospital, I remained unable to eat anything. My swollen spleen was pushing against my stomach, causing me to throw-up everything I ate. The spleen creates and stores red blood cells, and when red blood cells get trapped in the spleen, it becomes damaged. Now, Sickle Cell Disease was adding another painful condition for me to endure.

My doctors said I could only be released if my red blood cell count went up, but it couldn't go up if I couldn't eat. Nurses gave me juice and broth, trying to feed nourishment into my body. They kept oxygen masks over my face, pushing oxygen into my lungs to enrich my blood. My spleen continued to enlarge, trapping more red blood cells, consequently reducing my red blood count even more.

My blood count is usually 11, but it had been 7.0 when I was admitted to the hospital and after two blood transfusions, it was still only 7.5. (A normal hemoglobin red blood count is 21.) I was unbelievably distraught. I knew if I couldn't actually eat, I wouldn't make any progress. My doctor told me that if my blood cell count hadn't gone up by morning, I'd have to get a third transfusion.

I hated getting blood transfusions. Though I knew the chance of getting AIDS or hepatitis was slim, I had never liked the idea of someone else's blood in my body. Rick, understanding my distress, was supportive but firm. "You've got to eat if you want to get your blood count up!" he stressed. I knew he was right but my body was working against me. Everything I ate came up.

Despite feeling queasy, I decided to toughen up; I started to eat crackers slowly. After holding down a few crackers, Rick ordered me everything on the menu. Nurses happily sent the menu to the kitchen. When the food arrived I felt nauseous from the smell, but I pressed on gulping everything in sight. As I prayed to God, I ate a hamburger, French fries, pancakes, bacon, toast, steak with mashed potatoes with gravy. I ate whatever Rick handed me. I was determined to avoid another transfusion, and I prayed to not throw up.

And somehow, I managed not to. Early the next morning, when the nurse came in to take my blood, I was already dressed and ready to go home. "Where do you think you're going?" she asked. "I know my blood count went up," I said. "I'm going home." She looked doubtful, but gently drew out my rich red blood, which I knew now was full of nutrients.

I waited three hours for the results. When the doctor came into my room he laughed, seeing me fully dressed, still attached to a glucose IV, with tennis shoes hanging off the bed. "Your blood count went up to 10.5," he said, then paused. "I guess you can go home." Rick and I cheered and gave each other a high-five.

Looking back, damaging my spleen and spending a week in the hospital was a terribly stressful way to end a wonderful graduation celebration. But though desperate conditions were the outcome, it's still funny to think of myself gobbling enough food for a family of four.

When I think back on the trip, I don't think about the mini-stroke or swollen spleen. I think about wolfing down French toast, a hamburger, and a steak all in one sitting—then holding out my arm for the nurse to take my blood, knowing that this time, I'd defeated my illness simply by being a pig.

15
FORGIVING

I remember the day I forgave my mother. It was on her 70th birthday. Grace and I had taken her to a fine restaurant for dinner. She was so accustomed to living and eating like a poor woman, she became uncomfortable as we approached the seaside restaurant's valet parking.

Marina Del Rey was an upscale beach community of Los Angeles with relaxed yet trendy restaurants of every kind. As we drove into the driveway, parking attendants rushed to open our doors. My mother was distraught. "This place is too expensive," she said, while climbing out of the car. Grace and I winked at each other as we ushered her into the lobby of the dimly lit place.

My mother wore a glittery rainbow hat on top of her head, personally decorated with every color stone placed in too many places. The glimmering hat bounced colors off of every dim light in the room. With her usual black pant and blouse outfit, her glimmering hat sat on top of her head like a crown.

The restaurant was full of stylish professionals out for a mid-week dinner. Even though the lights were dim, I could see everyone notice my mother's hat, smiling as they looked away. This was nothing new. Whenever I took my mother out, her outlandish behavior and negative attention followed. I welcomed moving away from the front door, ignoring quiet snickers as we were led to our seats on the patio.

At the tables near us, I could hear soft dinner conversation. On queue, my mother began to speak loudly about prices, menu items, and how uncomfortable she felt with us spending money. Grace and I smiled, trying to keep the dinner conversation light, hoping for no trouble. When drinks came I swallowed my drink in one gulp. I was going to have a long night and needed Gallo wine to help me through it.

My mother watched as I placed a napkin across my lap, beginning to eat my salad with the salad fork. She looked around the room at the sophisticated setting and nearly yelled, "I can't believe I'm 70!" Grace and I both choked at the volume of her voice. Trying to calm her down, we both spoke quietly, begging, "Mom, please keep your voice down."

My mother took her napkin, dropped it on her lap, and picked up the entrée fork. While she ate her salad, I watched her face. Wrinkled, yet smooth for her age. Her face never showed much joy, but I could see a glimmer of pride as our main course arrived. "You two are professionals!" she beamed as a large hot plate of food was placed before her. For the first time, I felt my mother acknowledge that Grace and I had done well in our lives.

At that moment, I also felt pity for my mother. Seventy years had passed and she never really lived. At the hand of others or of her own, she struggled her whole life. Poverty was all she knew. It felt comfortable to her. This restaurant felt foreign. She couldn't get comfortable eating at a fine restaurant, even if somebody else was paying. I felt sorry for all her lost years.

I looked at my mother with new eyes. I saw an entire life of regrets, wasted on hate and self-pity. I felt sorry for how she'd missed out on the joys of life. Simple pleasures; like eating out with her daughters, or having thanksgiving dinner with all her children present. My mother had missed so much living, while holding on to anger. I watched my mother as she chewed with her mouth open. I understood that no one taught her proper manners because no one had showed me.

At that moment, during her 70th birthday dinner, I forgave my mother for everything she'd done. For those dark nights when I cried in pain, being ridiculed and ignored. For every embarrassing moment she seemed to take pleasure in. For every hug I'd not received. For every smile withheld.

I forgave my mother for being the victim. I forgave her for punishing her children and breaking family ties that were never bound to begin with. I forgave her for hating my father, a hate that did more damage to her than him. I forgave her for being imperfect, uneducated, and poor. I forgave it all.

Dinner continued with my mother speaking too loudly, causing others to smile politely. Grace and I bared it all, knowing it wouldn't last long. We ordered a large piece of cheese cake and happily indulged to celebrate this special event.

After dinner, I drove her home, said goodnight and went home to my waiting children. When I got home I kissed my daughter and promised to never be anything like my mother.

After that night, sometimes my mother would still pick a fight, bringing up some things I did as a child. I'd try different techniques to see which ones worked best at defusing conflict. At first, I just let her talk, ignoring negative comments. Then, I cut her off in mid-sentence, leading the conversation to a lighter note.

Sometimes, she would try to make me relive the tortures of *my* past. Reviewing abuse I endured or the torment of my children being separated. I would let her tell the negative version of the story. If she exaggerated, I corrected her. I didn't make excuses for my bad choices, bad behavior or mistakes. Unlike her, I could face my past without being bound by it.

After my mother had a stroke a few years later, I saw an unusually vulnerable side. Normally, a tough hard-shell of a woman, I saw her actually need people. Most of my sisters and brothers ran for the hills, not offering help or money for her care. It didn't surprise me. I'd seen this before with my father's death. Grace and I got together and worked out the details of the help she needed. In no time, she was on her feet again raising hell and taking names.

After her stroke, my mother began to reflect on *her* life. Every Sunday I'd call and we'd talk for hours. I listened patiently as she recounted a life of torment. When she got stuck on a topic, like my father, I gently prod her on to a better subject. I prod her with a gentle hand of love, a hand of pity. In order to have a relationship with her, I had to be able to listen and love.

Our relationship was a work in progress. In our long talks on Sunday, she would never take accountability for the part she played in the damage to our family. She didn't think she did anything wrong. She saw herself as the victim; everyone else was a casualty of her war.

In forgiving my mother, I had to forgive everything and everybody in my life. I would be justified to carry a torch of anger for all the pain I've endured, but I won't.

I could be mad at society for its exclusionary racism. Racism thrust upon me from both sides, being considered too black for some and not black enough for others. I was faced with this dichotomy my whole life. At work it came up, co-workers noting I was the only black person in the office. It came up at home, black friends and classmates calling me names like high-yellow and light-bright-almost-white. This clearly was insanity.

I could be outraged at my father for producing a brood of children, with a woman he stopped loving (or never loved to begin with). Years of his non-support, that caused many hungry days and endless hungry nights. I could be upset for his lack of love. He never acknowledged birthdays, holidays, or me. Since his religion didn't believe in Christmas, I never got to experience the joy of opening a gift from my father. My father was a complete stranger to me; even though I paid to give him a proper burial.

I could be displeased with my brothers and sisters for being flawed survivors like me. They scattered from a life of suffering, leaving behind no resemblance of a family. They watched as others suffered, yet never coming together to support or encourage those left behind. All of them victims of the same loveless childhood, to this day still scattered and fragile.

I could be disappointed with neighbors who saw my suffering; watching, uninvolved and unsympathetic as my sisters and I wore dirty, torn, clothes and always looked hungry. It wasn't their problem. Living in the ghetto made everyone a little selfish. I lived alongside desperate people trying to dodge the same bullet.

I could be outraged at my inner-city school education. It gave me the message, "You can't," when I knew I could. It didn't challenge me to do better, or to be better. Instead, it showed me negative differences. Asian kids were promoted to college while black kids were pushed aside. White schools got books while black schools got handouts. Teachers were afraid to teach us, never impressing the excitement of learning. The inequities of this education are still evident in my daily life.

I could loathe myself for making one bad decision after another. What the hell was I thinking getting married at seventeen? I could kick myself for every stupid thing I allowed. Forgetting I'm special and deserve to be treated with love and respect. And, for letting my children suffer, being transported from one house to another. The list could be endless if I ponder too long. I could emphasize all my flaws, magnifying them for everybody to see. What does that benefit?

136

I could detest my body, the part of myself that is weak, with unfit blood. While others ran, I sat. While others laughed, I cried. Pain, never far away, prodded me to suffer. I could cry till the end of my days, wallowing in a pit of self pity. God knows I have good cause.

Then, I could hate my mother, the only person in the world who is *supposed* to love me. Her cold unloving hand was all I knew. She didn't protect me at night while I rode buses to and from work. She punished me for crimes my father committed, calling herself the victim. She turned my family against themselves, causing them to hate even their own last name. She inflicted spiritual wounds in each and every one of my brothers and sisters, wounds that seem to be eternal. My mother passed her tormented life on to her innocent children, never understanding the generational damage.

A long time ago, I chose to forgive them all, a choice that didn't need their permission. I visualized the forgiveness Jesus had for all who abused him. He forgave those who didn't deserve it. The people I forgave didn't deserve it, couldn't earn it and surely couldn't give it back. I gave them forgiveness for free because it was a gift to myself.

I resolved to not carry the weight of anger and resentment like my mother. There was too much past, too much pain, and forgiving freed me. Once I decided to forgive them, bad memories simply faded, being replaced with hope. Forgiving allowed me to face my fears, leaving the baggage of self-pity behind, and replacing pain with joy.

Today, I choose my battles. Sometimes, my family will hurt me with undeserved coldness or unwarranted criticism. I don't stand for mistreatment, but I understand the source of their confusion. I go back to that place of forgiveness and pass them a portion once again. Where I abide, I have an endless supply.

16
LET GO

Four years after her first stroke, my mother had multiple "silent" heart attacks. They were silent because she didn't tell anyone about them.

On a routine visit, while passing through town to take care of other business, I noticed my mother looked frail and un-kept. I offered to take her out to dinner at a nearby diner, and as she gathered herself up, I noticed she couldn't walk without taking breaks to sit down.

As we walked toward the diner's entrance she complained, "My back hurts!" Since I was the family expert on pain, I told her about my pain reduction remedies. She grunted and looked unconcerned.

During dinner she asked unrelated questions like, "Do you throw-up when you have a cold?" I was confused. While talking with my mother, being confused was nothing new. Often times she had a habit of talking *at* you rather than *to* you. "Yes, sometimes I do." I told her.

After dinner we drove back to her apartment, with more unrelated questions about diarrhea, sweating, and dizziness. I told her, "You need to go to the doctor!" "I have an appointment on Monday!!" she said, disturbed by my prodding into her business. "OK," I said, "I'll call you Tuesday and see how it went." She grunted and got out of the car.

On Tuesday I called. My mother fumbled the phone as she picked the receiver up. "What did the doctor say?" I asked, fully expecting that she had a full report. "I didn't go." she said. "Why?" I asked, hoping that he rescheduled or something. "I've been throwing-up all day," she said. "I couldn't go."

I instantly got mad. Ever since I was a child this woman has been the angry boss of her own life. Especially after her second divorce she said, "No one is gonna tell me what to do again!" Well, I was sick and tired of this strong-willed, 87 year old woman, who was home alone throwing up.

I yelled into the phone, "You better call Silvia and have her take you to the hospital or I'm gonna call an ambulance from my home!" I lived 3 ½ hours away, but I was very willing to get that ball rolling. "Ok," she said very gently, then hung up.

I waited for 10 minutes and called back. When she answered the phone she knew it was me. "I called Silvia and she's gonna take me to the hospital," she said. "Ok, I'll keep in touch," I said, with a kinder voice than before. For the first time in her life, my mother followed my instructions.

I immediately got on the phone to call my sisters. This was an emergency and even though my mother was reluctant to get treatment, I knew something else was going on. Thinking about the odd, unrelated questions, and "back pain" and throwing-up, I knew this was serious.

After hearing the hospital admitted my mother with a heart valve that worked only 10%, I rushed to make the 3½ hour drive. When I got to the hospital the nursing staff would not talk to me. "What are her treatment options?" I asked. The nurses kept saying, "Your mother is competent to make her own decisions, we cannot talk to you about her treatment decisions." I was confused. "What?" I said. "Who's saying she's not competent?" I asked. They just shrugged their shoulders and moved on.

Again, in dealing with my mother, I was confused. I found out later that my mother had instructed nursing staff AND her doctors that her family was crazy and that they (me included) would try to force her to do things against her will. Hence, they released my mother (to her home) without treatment or any in-home aides like a wheelchair. This is after having multiple heart attacks and a heart valve only working 10%.

As they wheeled her out of her room, to the elevator, and to accounting to settle expenses, I was in a daze. I could not believe what was happening. Once again, my mother dictated all of the events, even if they could ultimately kill her. Then, they loaded her into a car and she was driven home.

Instinctually, I offered to spend the first night with her until we, as a family, figured out what to do. The first night was sheer hell. I watched as she'd breath and then stop, only to start back panting faster. She kicked her leg as if her heart was pushing a beat out with her foot. I was traumatized.

The next morning I argued with anyone who would listen. "She cannot be alone!" All night I had watched her fight for every breath and I could not let her live or die alone. This however was her biggest nightmare, needing anyone. She argued back, giving any lame reason for being alone. She fought with her last bit of strength, but I had seen the truth. She was unable to care for herself, use the restroom, walk without falling, and breathe.

With reluctance, she agreed to spend a few days with Silvia. Those few days ended with another hospital stay, and her doctor's figuring out that she was fighting an uphill battle alone. She was trying to fight to stay independent when her body was saying, "enough!" This was her last battle and in reality she was only fighting herself. Everyone else was trying to help her.

With a heart valve working only 10% the prognosis was not good. My mother was terminal with only a few months expected to live. She refused the only treatment option of having a pacemaker put in, so the doctor's sent her to a nursing home to live out her days. This was also one of her fears; being left alone in a nursing home with strangers in control.

A few weeks passed, I returned home and family members began to visit the nursing home. Grace, the baby of the family, who worked with the elderly at nursing homes, could not get over the dread on our mother's face. We both knew this was the ultimate torture to her. Grace took it upon herself to fight for what she knew was available for terminal patients, hospice care. This would allow our mother to go home with Grace, and have nursing care available at her home.

Needless to say, hospice care was a blessing. It was the most dignified way to live, when you were given a short life expectancy. My mother received daily in-home nursing care, medicine delivered, and home health aides who cared for and bathed her. She was treated with respect and love.

I witnessed my mother transform from a sneaky, mean, "don't tell me what to do" woman, to a kind and gentle soul. Her transformation began months before during our Sunday conversations, but from the first hospital stay in April to August, I noticed an amazing change. Each month I traveled the 3 ½ hour drive and stay a week to help relieve nursing staff at night and dispense medicine.

I'd also sit with my mother and watch T.V. We'd talk about God, or my children, or good food. It was a special time for my mother and me. Then, I'd watch visitors come and she'd receive them with kindness and love. I witnessed a transformation I prayed for all my life.

I prayed that my mother would see that people could love her and she could love them in return. I prayed that she would forgive the hurts of her past and allow others to forgive her. I prayed that she could find the peace of God, where gentleness and humbleness give rest. I prayed that she would not die that bitter old woman with hate driving her every scheme. My prayers were answered.

My mother forgave everyone, even those who did nothing wrong. She made peace with her children and her children made peace with her. I knew my mother was miserable trapped to a hospital bed. I believe she made peace with the world and was just waiting for God to do His part.

After a weeks stay, I returned home to take care of myself in between those stressful visits. While at home I got a call from Grace. "Mom had another stroke," she said. It was about eight o-clock at night and Rick was not home. I live in the mountains where there are few road lights, so me driving alone at that time was ridiculous. "I'm coming now," I said, then hung up the phone.

I started packing as Rick called me. "How you doing?" he asked. In one breath I answered, "My mother had a stroke. I'm packing now and I'm driving to LA in a few minutes." Rick paused a moment, thinking about what I was saying, and I guess, understanding that I was crazy. "No," he said, "You're not driving tonight. You'll wait till the morning!" I instantly got mad. How the hell is he gonna tell me I'm not going? Then, I thought about it. I am not well myself, it is dark, and it's a 3 ½ hour drive, what am I thinking? "Ok," I said. "I'll see you in the morning and I'll drive then."

The next day I drove to Grace's house and sure enough my mother had a second stroke. The first day she could not speak, but had some coherence. She was able to slightly respond with a gentle squeeze. I immediately began my normal duties as relief nurse and medicine dispenser. This time my mother needed 24 hour care.

I had to be very careful during this stay because I did not have enough time to recover from the previous visit. I had to prevent myself from ending up in the hospital with some stress related sickle cell 'crisis'. So, I made sure Grace understood I could not stay more than a week. She spoke with the head hospice nurse and they assured her that more nursing staff would be assigned.

Three days later, around ten p.m., I had to give my mother her last dose of medicine for the day. I filled the syringe as I had always done. I drew the medicine into the syringe, checking the dosage twice, and then leaned over my mother's sleeping face. The night duty nurse could not dispense medicine, so I asked her to help me lift my mothers head and open her mouth.

I gently placed the syringe into her limp mouth, pushing the "comforting" medicine under her tongue. The clear liquid seeped into her mouth. I wiped her moist lips, laid her head gently on the pillow and turned away from her limp, frail body.

Grace, who worked swing shift, called and said she was on her way home. The night duty nurse sat reading a magazine until her shift was over. At eleven, she left and I prepared the room for the night. I turned off the fan, opened the window to a small crack, turned the night-light on, and checked my mother one final time.

My daughter, knowing her grandmother wasn't doing well, also came to spend the night. Before I finished checking things, she ran into the room and scared me. "I forgot to say goodnight," she said, running past me. She leaned over her grandmother, whispered something in her ear, and kissed her face.

I looked around the room one final time and walked out. I laid down to take a short break before Grace would come home to relieve me. Grace was delayed because of traffic. I dozed off waiting for her. When Grace came into the room yelling, my daughter and I jumped up into the air. Together, we all ran to our mother's room where she laid.

My mother waited until after my final room check and before Grace came home from work. No one was with her to disturb or fuss over her. Finally, my mother would let go of everything. Quietly, and alone at midnight, she went home to be with the Lord.

It was a beautiful ending to an un-beautiful life. God blessed my mother one final time and He blessed my family to see her at peace, finally.

17
LOOKING FORWARD

Back when I was ten-years old and the doctor told me I would only live to be thirty-years old, I thought that was forever. After blowing out candles on my 30th birthday cake, I could only think about Sickle Cell Disease having a birthday, too. As everyone sang "Happy Birthday," dread, instead of joy, filled my day. I could only think of this as being my grand finale.

Fast forward twenty years, at fifty, I've passed that dreaded birthday death sentence. I consider every day after that birthday a miracle, a marvel, and a blessing. Most studies show the life expectancy for a person with Sickle Cell Disease to be 42 for males, and 48 for females. I am living past that life expectancy and looking toward new possibilities, not at my end.

I have made peace with this thing living inside me. Though my life has had its ups and downs, I always chose to live past my pain. Rather than simply carry the baggage of the difficult parts, I gathered up pieces of joy along the way. Yes, my disease is speaking more loudly these days. Its demands cannot be ignored. But now, my body has my full attention.

I often ask myself how I managed. How did I not crumble and succumb to pills or drugs? How did I not consider suicide a solution? Well, the body is an incredible thing. It can crumble in the face of disease, but it can also adapt. In my case, I was resilient enough to adapt to my hardship, not give in to it. I developed a high tolerance for pain, and faced the fear of it fearlessly. This gave me the power, simply, to live.

I know there is little chance I will live to see a cure for Sickle Cell Disease in my lifetime. But I am an optimist at heart, and I have hope for others. Children born with Sickle Cell Disease today have more prospects for a cure.

Innovations in stem cell research and better bone marrow transplants are in the horizon. There is hope for their future, and I cheer them on from the sidelines. My next step is not a cure, but simply to put one foot in front of the other, to take one breath, and then another.

To that end, I believe there are ways I can continue to help myself even without the use of a life-saving drug. I continue to eat well, take vitamins and herbs, and use natural health remedies to prolong my life. I've found herbal teas to help me naturally with pain, and I use minerals to strengthen my bones. I use herbal creams to reduce swelling and soothe pain, too.

I also nurture my creative side in order to support my emotional health. I have started writing for newspapers and magazines. My father-in-law sometimes teases me that I simply write to vent. But I want to tell my story to others to lay the way for them to overcome as well.

As I write the story of my life, I see I have been strong for a long time. When I felt fear, I found courage in God. When I felt insecure, I turned to my intellect. When I felt hunger, I got a job. Whatever life threw at me, I didn't cower or feel sorry for myself. I took a bat to it. We can all agree that disease means a life of hardship. But so what! Life sometimes hurts. When you are in pain, you can't wallow in it.

Whenever I looked past my pain there was always unexpected blessings: a compassionate stranger, a teacher who acknowledged my talents, an unexpected friend. Though it often felt as if life was trying to tear me down, if I looked around, I could see that others, throughout my life, were building me up.

Many times, I was ashamed of my disease, and I wished it away simply because it made me different. I was ashamed of being poor, being hungry, being from such a large family. I was ashamed that, in contrast to my friends' loving homes, my family didn't even like

150

each other. In short, I was ashamed of all things I couldn't help.

But now I've learned that my shame was useless. None of these things were my fault. It was simply life, with all of its imperfections and challenges. I learned what is beyond your control should never be a source of shame to you. Instead, you must deal with it—and try to make the best of what you've been given. Whatever else it hands you; life still gives you the freedom to accept yourself.

This book is my offering to people living with Sickle Cell Disease and a testament to overcoming it. It is my way to say, "I understand your pain and I understand your fears, because I have had them, too."

My entire life, people were scared that I would spread Sickle Cell Disease to them. That was their ignorance. Because of my upbringing, people undervalued me, not expecting me to rise above my environment. That was their foolishness.

People even gave me flack for trying to manage my disease, for worrying about things like elevation, heat, or cold—for simply saying, "I need to rest." Those people don't understand what it's like to live with sickle cell. Those people take wellness for granted. But I know that my ability to walk, to eat, to see, and hear is a big deal.

I am grateful for every one of my senses: but most of all, the power to think. It allows me to remember that simply being alive is a very big deal.

Today, I am doing well. I still have my original hips, and I don't plan on having replacements any time soon. My spleen remains swollen, and sometimes affects my digestion.

However, I always endure. I am able to do most things, within reason, and my life is happy and fulfilling. I have a husband who loves me, children who make me proud, an extended family that, though not perfect, supports me, as well as plenty of friends. I've got a lot.

My dancing days are over. My body no longer flows with the rhythm of whatever is playing. Sometimes it resists any movement at all. If I push too hard and try a bend or stretch, it pays me back with weeks of swelling and pain. When I hear a melody, I still sway to the beat in my mind.

When I see someone else dance, I remember feeling the wave of flowing movements. As their muscles stretch, I imagine my muscles stretching, too. When they point their toes, I feel my own feet flex. Sickle Cell Disease has taken dance from me, but when I watch someone else do it, I still feel their joy.

As my children are now adults, they comprehend my condition and are very attentive to me. They both gently listen with compassion, as I tell them of my physical limitations. They encourage me to live well and live long.

While they were growing up, I never let them see me suffer from a 'crisis.' At the time, they had no idea what my suffering really looked like. I purposely hid that suffering from their view. When I would get sick, I'd send them to relatives not wanting to scare them with the details. As time passes; I allow my children to see my vulnerability. I have to be honest with them about my limitations.

My immediate family is still disjointed. Unable to overcome the tragedy of an abused childhood, my sisters and brothers exist in separate worlds. I connect with some of them, in small indirect ways.

My hope for them is through their children. Their wounds apparently are too deep and unforgiving too heal. My nieces and nephews, whom I call "third generation", they are my hope. Without current scars, I'm hopeful this generation will connect. Putting their parents past behind *them*, I'm hopeful these young relatives will give family a try.

Looking forward, I am hopeful, as usual. Although, my life has been molded by the imperfection of my body, I refuse to give in to self-pity. I still fight to overcome limitations, by doing my part to stay well. I look for ways to worship the perfect God, who made everything perfectly, including me.

Pain and I are still constant companions. Since we first met on that living room floor-heater, we remain joined at the hip, literally to this day. Sometimes, I do cry at night. Pain really hurts. In the morning, however, I dry my eyes and start over again.

I look forward to seeing grandchildren, loving them in a spoil rotten kind of way. I look forward to living to a ripe old age; with beautiful wrinkles on my face, gray hair (without Miss Clairol), and a rocking chair with my beloved Rick beside me.

I look forward to this book touching people's hearts and minds, encouraging those who must overcome adversity, as well. No matter what life has in store for me. I say bring it on. I look forward to it all.

18
ORPHAN DISEASE

In 1930, American doctor Dr. Lemuel Whitley Diggs suggested pain in sickle cell patients is due to sickle cells clogging up small blood vessels (found during autopsies). At the time, further investigation of causes by the American medical community was unpopular and unfunded because people afflicted were of African decent. In 1949, another American, Dr. Linus Paulin discovered that abnormal hemoglobin was the cause of Sickle Cell Disease, but twenty-two years would pass before nationally funded research was approved.

In 1972, the Sickle Cell Control Act was passed by President Nixon to publicly fund screening, research and treatment for people with sickle cell disease. Finally, the American medical community would take the lead in research and treatment for people with sickle cell disease, and this was about the time I received my first care.

To write this book, I researched global databanks to see what the world knew or thought about this disease. I was shocked and appalled at what I uncovered.

In America, I discovered Sickle Cell Disease is identified as an "orphan disease." According to the definition outlined by United States National Institute of Health, an orphan disease is "a rare disease considered to have a prevalence of fewer than 200,000 affected individuals in the United States. Certain diseases with 200,000 or more affected individuals may be included in this list, if certain subpopulations *(I think they mean ethnic)* have the disease are equal to the prevalence standard for rare diseases."

The American pharmaceutical community agreed when they concluded, this number of patients was just too low to have been 'adopted' for further research because it provided little financial incentive for the private sector to make and market new medications to treat or prevent it. This was concluded, even though the Orphan Drug Act of 1983 offered financial incentives to companies to encourage development of drugs to treat orphan diseases.

With America taking the lead in treatment and care; sickle cell disease is still considered an orphan disease. This step-child designation has fueled misinformation, medical racism, and limited drug treatments. Even though America is ahead of the world related to sickle cell disease education and treatments, the view is blinded by misinformation regarding who it affects its complications, the world-wide impact, and the suffering it causes.

In 2007, at a World Health Organization (WHO) meeting in Cyprus, global health professionals analyzed their countries independent management of hemoglobin disorders and submitted their findings in a final report. Their global findings and statistics were shocking. The number of people suffering from sickle cell disease, and the related Thalassemia blood disorder, was epidemic in some countries (4).

The statistics gathered for this report were based on a few standard elements related to sickle cell disease (SCD) and Thalassemia. The countries in attendance reported on; number/ percent of population affected, type of care offered (if any), prevention/education offered, treatment offered, birth rate (if known), and care limitations.

As I read the results of this report I cried. There were twenty countries that reported; with South-East Asia, Western Europe and the Middle East being lumped together as if they were three small counties, instead of many little countries. Of the twenty countries reported, only seven had Sickle Cell Disease/ Thalassemia Care Programs. The number of people suffering from sickle cell disease (SCD) and the related Thalassemia was as follows (see table 1):

Africa – 25% of total population has SCD, high infant mortality, no national care.

Belgium - 1.8% Thalassemia in one city alone, no national care or measure.

Brazil – 1 in 35 carriers, high complication mortality, education only, limited care.

Canada – No national testing, no SCD measure/care/treatment, some Thalassemia data.

Egypt – Thalassemia 1000/1.5 mil births, SCD 22% in desert communities, no SDC care.

France – 5% in Paris alone, only "ethnic" testing, 285 new SCD per year, some care.

Germany – No measure, no care.

Greece – 17% of pop. with Thalassemia, no SCD treatment/care, prevention is target.

India – up to 97% are carriers, care/treatment provided, overwhelmed & epidemic.

Jamaica – 47% of population has SCD or trait, has good education/treatment/care.

Lebanon – 71% children with Thalassemia, registed and tracked, no SCD treatment/care.

Middle East – Thalassemia/SCD # unknown, high infant mortality, no SCD treatment/care.

Sri Lanka - No SCD measure, 5% of 20 million are Thalassemia carriers, no treatment.

South East Asia – 60 types of Thalassemia, 82% of new births, no SCD measure, epidemic.

Spain – SCD 1/5000 new births, only test "at risk", no Thalassemia test, limited care.

United Kingdom – No national care/treatment, only "target" testing, 50% die pre-35yr.

United States – 3 million carriers, 2,000 new births, has treatment and care available.

Table 1 - "Management of Haemoglobin Disorders". World Health Organization (WHO) 2008(4)

With these global numbers, how could sickle cell disease, and its related blood disorder Thalassemia, be called orphan?

The World Health Organization's report verifies sickle cell disease and Thalassemia are not being managed. They are the cause of increased infant mortality (pre- 5 years), result in high rates of disability, and are becoming a global "epidemic."

According to a World Health Organization's (WHO) Genes and Human Diseases report, the source of Sickle Cell Disease is DNA (Deoxyribonucleic Acid). DNA is the blueprint of life and has the instructions for making each and every one of us. The report states, "Pure genetic diseases are caused by a single error in a single gene in the human DNA" (3).

These single gene errors are called "monogenic diseases" and affect millions of people worldwide. Scientists estimate that over 10,000 human diseases are known to be monogenic. Besides Sickle Cell Disease, other monogenic diseases are: Thalassaemia, Haemophilia, Cystic Fibrosis, Tay Sachs disease, Fragile X syndrome (cause of retardation), and Huntington's disease (3). Each one of these diseases cause suffering and death to millions of people.

To better describe sickle cell blood disorders, the Sickle Cell Information Center at Emory University School of Medicine provides a clinical definition. This definition will also explain why the World Health Organization measures Sickle Cell Disease along with Thalassemia (7).

"Sickle Cell Disease is a group of inherited red blood cell disorders. Normal red blood cells are round like doughnuts, and they move through small blood tubes in the body to deliver oxygen. Sickle red blood cells become hard, sticky and shaped like sickles used to cut wheat. When these hard and pointed red cells go through the small blood tube, they clog the flow and break apart. This can cause pain, damage and a low blood count, or anemia.

What makes the red cell sickle?

There is a substance in the red cell called hemoglobin that carries oxygen inside the cell. One little change in this substance causes the hemoglobin to form long rods in the red cell when it gives away oxygen. These rigid rods change the red cell into a sickle shape instead of the round shape.

How do you get Sickle Cell Disease, anemia or the trait?

You inherit the abnormal hemoglobin from your parents, who may be carriers of the sickle cell trait or

160

parents with sickle cell disease. You can not catch it. You are born with the sickle cell hemoglobin and you have it for life. If you inherit only one sickle gene, you have sickle cell "trait". If you inherit two sickle cell genes you have sickle cell disease.

What is sickle cell trait?

Normal hemoglobin is called type A. Sickle hemoglobin is called type S. Sickle Cell trait is the presence of hemoglobin AS. A person with Sickle Cell trait is a person who carries only one inherited sickle hemoglobin (S) gene, and one inherited normal hemoglobin (A) gene. Other hemoglobin traits common in the United States are AC and AE traits. All of these traits could show signs of Sickle Cell complications, like sickness at high altitudes and anemia.

Are there different types of sickle cell disease?

There are three common types of sickle cell disease in the United States: Hemoglobin SS or Sickle Cell Anemia, Hemoglobin SC or Sickle Cell Disease, and Hemoglobin sickle beta-Thalassemia. Each of these can cause sickle pain episodes and complications, but some are more common than others.

Is Sickle Cell only in African Americans?

Sickle cell is in many nationalities including African Americans, Africans, Arabs, Greeks, Italians, Latin Americans, and those from India. You can be Caucasian and have sickle cell disease or trait. All races should be screened for this hemoglobin at birth.

How can I be tested?

A simple blood test called the hemoglobin electrophoresis can be done by your doctor or local sickle cell foundation. This test will tell if you are a carrier of the sickle cell trait or if you have the disease.

Newborn Screening

Most States now perform the sickle cell test when babies are born. The simple blood test will detect sickle cell disease or sickle cell trait. Other types of traits that may be discovered include: Hemoglobin C trait, Hemoglobin E trait, Hemoglobin Barts, which indicates an Alpha Thalassemia trait, and Beta Thalassemia trait.

What are the complications of having sickle cell?

Complications from the (sticky) sickle cells blocking blood flow and early breaking apart include:

1. pain episodes

2. strokes
3. increased infections
4. leg ulcers
5. bone damage
6. yellow eyes or jaundice
7. early gallstones
8. lung blockage
9. Kidney damage and loss of body water in urine.
10. painful erections in men (priapism)
11. blood blockage in the spleen or liver (sequestration)
12. eye damage
13. low red blood cell counts (anemia)
14. delayed growth

What can be done to help prevent these complications?

Sickle cell patients should be under the care of a medical team that understands sickle cell disease. All newborn babies detected with sickle cell disease should be placed on daily penicillin to prevent serious infections. All of the childhood immunizations should be given plus the flu vaccine. Parents should know how to check for a fever because this signals the need for a quick medical check-up for serious infection.

The following are general guidelines to keep the sickle cell patient healthy:

1. Taking the vitamin folic acid (folate) daily to help make new red cells.
2. Daily penicillin until age six to prevent serious infection.
3. Drinking plenty of water daily (8-10 glasses for adults).
4. Avoiding too hot or too cold temperatures
5. Avoiding over exertion and stress.
6. Get plenty of rest.
7. Get regular check-ups from knowledgeable health care providers.

Patients and families should watch for the following conditions that need an urgent medical evaluation:

1. Fever
2. Chest pain
3. Shortness of Breath
4. Increasing tiredness
5. Abdominal swelling
6. Unusual headache
7. Any sudden weakness or loss of feeling
8. Pain that will not go away with home treatment
9. Priapism (painful erection that will not go down)
10. Sudden vision change"

"What is Sickle Cell Disease". Sickle Cell Information Center-Emory University School of Medicine(7)

The definition of Sickle Cell Disease and its complications, and the WHO report confirms the shocking truth. People with this disease are suffering, not being treated, nor is care even being made available.

In America, people are being treated, care is offered and educational programs are in place to inform the public (ethnic populations) about prevention. With all this in place, ignorance still prevails.

Some young people with Sickle Cell Disease in American, I've been told by medical professionals, are "in denial" about their medical condition. These young people with Sickle Cell Disease try to live like everyone else, and as they do, they find themselves in the hospital time after time having episodes of pain, infection, lung dysfunction, low blood counts and needing blood transfusions.

In a New England Journal of Medicine report on the mortality of people with Sickle Cell Disease in the United States, the life expectancy for males is 42 years and 48 years for females (6). People with Sickle Cell Disease hear this statistic everyday of their lives, and the stigma of this looming over their heads can damper any hopes for a long life.

One Sickle Cell Specialist told me, some young people with Sickle Cell Disease give up on life. They conclude, "I'm dying anyway, so what the hell!" They don't take care of their bodies; they drink alcohol, and basically give up. Needless to say, mortality is high in these cases.

There are also high rates of depression among people with Sickle Cell Disease because chronic pain, disabilities, pain medication not working, and a host of real life challenges must be endured. Social stagnation and ignorance also cause many people with Sickle Cell Disease to hide their condition from friends and family, like I did, and they suffer alone. In addition, the high cost of medication and health care can cause illegal drug addiction and alcoholism.

In a 2000 American Journal of Epidemiology report by the Society for Epidemiologic Research, mortality rates for people with Sickle Cell Disease was measured during 1979-1995. Using data from the National Center for Health Statistics, 1 million deaths were reviewed, and anyone with sickle cell listed as cause of death was measured. The state-specific measurement totaled approximately 967 out of 1 million people died from Sickle Cell Disease (2).

These totals seem odd. The problem I have with these totals is that it measured "target" people specifically, some states had no information available at all, and the total population (the 1 million people who died) were not all tested for evidence of sickle cell disease/trait prior to death. Some of those people may have had the disease or trait, died from one of its many complications, and was not included in the Sickle Cell measurement. But what do I know?

Death caused by Sickle Cell Disease can not be fully measured because secondary complications like: osteoarthritis, stroke, heart disease, high blood pressure, viral infections, depressive disorders, lung dysfunction, *Polycythemia Vera of the* spleen or liver, anemia, alcohol or drug abuse are listed as cause of death. The origin of these deaths, however, could have been attributed to Sickle Cell Disease complications.

The Disease Control Project, which measured the global burden of disease and risk factors, did not measure Sickle Cell Disease along with diseases such as; osteoarthritis, stroke, heart disease, vision disorders, depressive disorders, lung dysfunction, anemia, alcohol or drug abuse (Measuring the Global Burden of Disease and Risk Factors 1). There really are no global statistics on the true impact of Sickle Cell Disease on our population.

People with Sickle Cell Disease become disabled early in life by one, if not all, of the associated complications. As a result, when people with Sickle Cell Disease age, they become afflicted with one or many of its complications, like I have. Based on my review of the American Journal of Preventive Medicine's report, Assessing the Burden of Disease in the United States Using Disability-Adjusted Life

<u>Years</u>, I could find no measurement of the specific number of people who die from the disabling affects of Sickle Cell Disease (McKenna 5).

What does all this information from these reports mean? In my view, these reports contain results that are based on limited measurements (like measuring Black people only). In addition, some of these reports are incomplete due to disconnected conclusions (like death by stroke, when it was really brought on by Sickle Cell Disease). No one knows how deeply rooted Sickle Cell Disease really is.

The World Health Organization is obtaining global measurements, and therefore, there's hope for better analysis of the true impact of Sickle Cell Disease on the world.

There is also hope for people living with Sickle Cell Disease, as information becomes more widely available. There is active research to find cures through stem cell possibilities, and bone marrow transplants. And, there is one drug, Hydroxyurea, which is an option available to help the body produce healthy fetal hemoglobin without the sickle cell abnormality. There are some side effects with this drug treatment, but it has shown promise to help many people.

There is also more education available about alternative health remedies to improve the quality of life. Herbs and supplements are being used to reduce infection, help ease pain, detoxify the blood, and aide all sorts of elements people endure.

Even with those shocking global statistics in the WHO's <u>Haemoglobin Disorders</u> report, the future is beginning to look bright (4). As the world takes off their blinders and takes a good look at testing, education, treatment and care for people with Sickle Cell Disease, medical racism will have to cease.

My personal conclusion about Sickle Cell Disease is that it's a human condition, not an African or ethnic condition. In my opinion, the "target" testing of ethnic groups, identified in the WHO report (7), is impractical. With racial mixing and immigration of nationalities, these blood disorders will eventually creep into everyone's blood. Testing should be standard for all newborns.

Dr. Martin Luther King Jr. said, "Our lives begin to end the moment we become silent about things that matter." I am just one of many voices crying out in the wilderness that Sickle Cell Disease (and its related blood disorder Thalassemia) is a condition where people of all nationalities are suffering and dying needlessly.

The End

LINKS

Ability Magazine – Dancing With Sickle Cell
www.abilitymagazine.com/sickle-cell-anemia.html

Our Voice –The Voice of people living with Sickle
Cell Disease
www.sicklecell-ourvoice.blogspot.com

Sickle Cell Disease Association of America
www.sicklecelldisease.org

Sickle Cell Information Center
www.scinfo.org

U.S. National Heart, Lung, Blood Institute
www.nhlbi.nih.gov/new/sicklecell.htm

Sickle Cell Society, London England
www.sicklecellsociety.org

ABOUT THE AUTHOR

Patient Expert Blogger Award winner, P. Allen Jones has been a long-time healthcare advocate for people suffering with sickle cell disease. As a health advocate blogger, Jones speaks to millions of people worldwide about the issues that confront people with sickle cell disease.

Featured in *Ability Magazine* (2009), the leading celebrity, health, disability and human potential magazine, Jones' life was profiled and Sickle Cell Disease finally got the national awareness it deserves.

As a featured writer for the Southern Sierra Messenger newspaper, Jones' article *"Ponder This"* offered poignant opinions on current events and politics.

Jones' article *"Ponder Faith"* was featured on the Women's National Book Association, Visalia Delta, and Tulare Times websites.

Educated in California, Jones studied finance, production operations and engineering. This diverse educational background led to a 22 year Federal executive career. Now retired from NASA, Jones works with various hospitals and universities to develop patient training and awareness programs for Sickle Cell Disease. P. Allen Jones lives in California, married with two children.

www.pallenjones.com